T0025045

A GUIDE TO AFTERLIFE COMMUNICATION

A GUIDE TO
Afterlife
COMMUNICATION

How to Heal from Loss and Connect with Your Loved Ones on the Other Side

AUDREY SLOAN TATE

ROCKRIDGE
PRESS

Copyright © 2021 by Rockridge Press, Emeryville, California

No part of this publication may be reproduced, stored in a retrieval system, or transmitted in any form or by any means, electronic, mechanical, photocopying, recording, scanning, or otherwise, except as permitted under Sections 107 or 108 of the 1976 United States Copyright Act, without the prior written permission of the Publisher. Requests to the Publisher for permission should be addressed to the Permissions Department, Rockridge Press, 6005 Shellmound Street, Suite 175, Emeryville, CA 94608.

Limit of Liability/Disclaimer of Warranty: The Publisher and the author make no representations or warranties with respect to the accuracy or completeness of the contents of this work and specifically disclaim all warranties, including without limitation warranties of fitness for a particular purpose. No warranty may be created or extended by sales or promotional materials. The advice and strategies contained herein may not be suitable for every situation. This work is sold with the understanding that the Publisher is not engaged in rendering medical, legal, or other professional advice or services. If professional assistance is required, the services of a competent professional person should be sought. Neither the Publisher nor the author shall be liable for damages arising herefrom. The fact that an individual, organization, or website is referred to in this work as a citation and/or potential source of further information does not mean that the author or the Publisher endorses the information the individual, organization, or website may provide or recommendations they/it may make. Further, readers should be aware that websites listed in this work may have changed or disappeared between when this work was written and when it is read.

For general information on our other products and services or to obtain technical support, please contact our Customer Care Department within the United States at (866) 744-2665, or outside the United States at (510) 253-0500.

Rockridge Press publishes its books in a variety of electronic and print formats. Some content that appears in print may not be available in electronic books, and vice versa.

TRADEMARKS: Rockridge Press and the Rockridge Press logo are trademarks or registered trademarks of Callisto Media Inc. and/or its affiliates, in the United States and other countries, and may not be used without written permission. All other trademarks are the property of their respective owners. Rockridge Press is not associated with any product or vendor mentioned in this book.

Interior and Cover Designer: Stephanie Sumulong
Art Producer: Sara Feinstein
Editor: Jed Bickman
Production Editor: Jenna Dutton
Production Manager: Holly Haydash

Illustrations used under license from Polar Vectors/Diana Hlevnjak

ISBN: Print   978-1-64876-651-0
        eBook 978-1-64876-151-5

R0

To the Divine Mother,
to my mother,
and to my mother's mother.
Thank you.

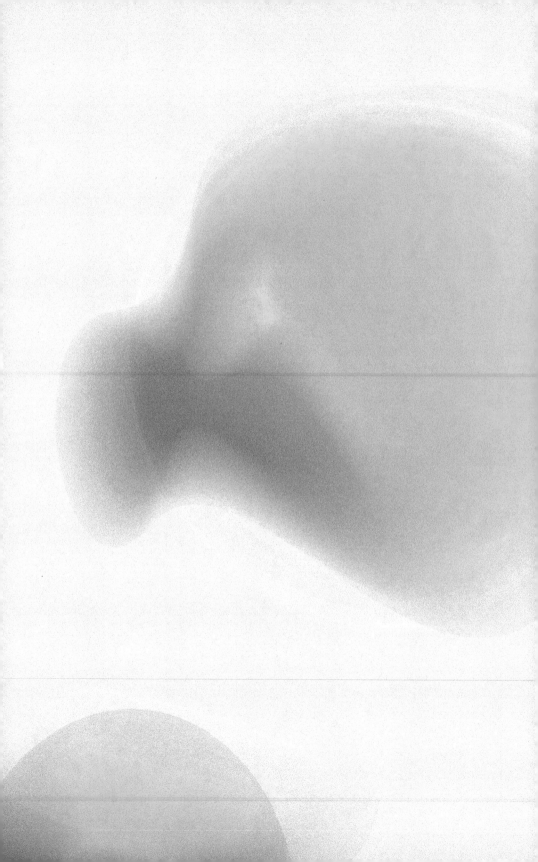

Contents

Introduction

Nothing can happen more beautiful than death.

—WALT WHITMAN, *LEAVES OF GRASS*

Welcome to a bigger picture of death. You have not found this book by accident. Wherever you are in your journey, you belong here. You are ready for this perspective to heal and ascend to a higher state of being where you can receive support from the deceased as you mourn your loved one.

Although my story is different from yours, I know the feeling of losing someone you love. It was nine years ago when it felt like my whole world came crumbling down—because it did. My great-grandmother, affectionately called Grams, was my first experience of loss. We were very close here on Earth, enjoying each other's company on a daily basis. She lived on a big horse farm that more than three generations had grown up on. Grams also was the matriarch and backbone of our extended family. After her passing, our once-close family, which had been bonded by Grams, fell apart without her presence. I felt alone and didn't know where to turn for support. Feeling depressed, I would sit in bed watching reruns of *Long*

Island Medium and revisit the "superpowers" I'd had as a child. I prayed to reignite the spiritual connections I once felt as a little girl on my family's horse farm. I wanted to hear from Grams and remember the innocent recognition of the spiritual realm.

I am a natural-born medium. I was brought into this world with the awareness that I had the ability to communicate with the deceased. A medium finds balance between the spiritual and material worlds. Some of us weave in and out of these worlds throughout different phases of our lives. This book will teach you the skills you need to stay centered so that you can thrive in both the spiritual world and the material world.

The painful loss of Grams drove me to inquire about what happens after we die. Her death inspired big questions in my life that people in my community didn't have answers for. My healing heart then led me to travel around the globe studying, listening, and learning from different experiences. I have been led to plant medicine and ayahuasca circles. I have kneeled at the altar of St. Peter's Basilica at the Vatican and have been blessed by Balinese priests in Indonesia. I have drunk the holy water of Brazilian healer John of God, I have held my breath, I have fasted, I have practiced yoga, and I have bowed down to deities and religious archetypes from all corners of the planet. I have sat in séances and table tippings (a form of mediumship) at the most prestigious spiritual college in the world, Arthur Findlay College. I have visited the most "haunted" places and traveled to more sacred lands than I can count on both hands. I have read books by and taken classes with premier mediums and spiritual leaders. I have also sat with hundreds upon hundreds of grieving clients who come to me to connect with the afterlife and activate their own spiritual powers. The learning still continues as the endless depth of the alternative realms continues to unravel only to reveal the correct nature of my naive human heart. The real wisdom is in knowing that nothing can fill the void of missing another human in their flesh.

In this book, I hand over the embodied wisdom that I have acquired through my personal journey of finding faith in a time of death. This book is your cheat sheet. Intuitively digest the information in whatever way your soul desires. It is not intended to be dogmatic in any form, nor does it adhere to any theological disposition. There is no spiritual practice here proven to heal your pain—only you know what is best for you. Take on the terminology lightly, as I have written this book with the intention of accommodating all backgrounds and beliefs. There is no "right way" to think about this information. At times, you may need to replace or exchange a term with a word that resonates more deeply with you, and that's okay. Hold on to the information you need and leave the rest behind. Get a new journal to take notes on both the information you read here and the experiences you have with the afterlife.

It is time to color outside the lines. If you feel like you may never see the light again, let these words hold you. Let the gentle sway of gravity from Mother Moon lift your worries and pain. This is your reminder that everything here is meant to serve your highest good. There is nothing wrong with you. This is not the light at the end of the tunnel; this is your instruction booklet on how to light that sucker up.

CHAPTER 1

Making Space for Your Grief

I decided to go for a hike on a local nature trail. When I arrived at the trailhead, I watched the last cell bar disappear on my phone. I shrugged it off and said, "I trust you, Spirit." As I hiked, I could feel my ancestors as my heart realigned with its true nature, and each turn I made was pure bliss. When I got back to my car, it was stuck in mud and would need to be towed. I said aloud, "Spirit, show me the purpose of this." Dusk was setting, and I didn't want to be alone out in the woods. I had one bar of service again and called a local tow-truck company. The person who answered happened to be right around the corner. "Thank you, Spirit," I said.

When the tow truck arrived, the driver and I both got out of our cars to greet each other in the last moments of daylight. Up walked this tough-looking man, and *whoosh* . . . I saw and felt a flash of light. He reached out his hand and said, "Hey, I'm Joe." The vulnerable channeled words from Spirit sat on my tongue, and my body felt like a live wire. He didn't look like the type who would openly cry, but I knew the message I had for him would bring him to his knees. I felt his emotions building up in my lungs.

"Hi, Joe. I am a medium," I said. He looked puzzled, but this couldn't wait. "I can communicate with people who have died. Do you mind if I share a message for you from your father?"

He said, "Okay, go on." A tear dropped from his eye before I even began. When I shared the personal message for him from his father, his head melted into his palms, and he murmured, "I do it all for him." The power of authenticity took hold of him, and he exploded into emotion. Joe explained that he had taken on his father's responsibilities, and though his family and business were thriving, he held grief in his heart, which was manifesting as physical ailments. Hearing from his father freed him of the pain he had been holding on to.

You've Suffered a Loss

Regardless of how recently we've experienced the loss of a loved one, grief has the ability to live within our bodies for lifetimes. The loss of someone may affect us in ways that we can't see on the surface. We may carry a burden of loss even when we feel as if we have moved on with our lives. Just like Joe's story, we, too, may ignore the emotions and healing process to a point at which they manifest as stress or physical ailments. This is because your body interprets grief as trauma. When experiencing the death of a loved one, you are a mirror of that loss. You, too, are experiencing your own death—a death of your old identities. However, death comes to remind the living to live. Death reminds us that there is a deeper meaning to life, a bigger picture than what we can see.

I know that grieving is not easy. Processing the emotions you feel after a loved one's death is not easy. In fact, many people don't face the pain they feel inside. Your grief process is as unique as your thumbprint or the rhythm of your heartbeat. It would be inhuman to not feel pain when a loved one dies. There is no quick solution for these emotions, but you can choose to be present with your process. Understand this concept so that you don't mask what is real as you move forward. Over time, you will gain allies and tools that will give you great skills to turn grief into its polarity of joy, but nothing can replace the absence of the physical presence of a passed loved one. Nothing in this book is meant to replace your loved one or negate your mourning process. I feel deeply for what you are experiencing and invite you to be compassionate with yourself during this journey.

Everyone's Process Is Different

In *Only Love Is Real: A Story of Soulmates Reunited*, Brian L. Weiss writes, "If you rely exclusively on the advice of others, you may make terrible mistakes. Your heart knows what you need. Other people have *other* agendas." This is important insight: Everyone's process of grief and mourning is different, and there is no "right way" to grieve. So throw out everything anyone has ever told you about how to grieve, including the "five stages of grief." Anyone who has ever experienced the gut-wrenching pain of losing a loved one knows there's no one-size-fits-all approach. While there may be different stages of healing, there is no direction or hierarchy to those stages. Your path is different from other people's paths. For this reason, be careful about comparing your story to others' stories to find answers. Your journey is yours, and it is sacred. Treat it as so.

What does it mean to make something sacred? It means seeing it with the perspective of connection; that we are cocreating with a collective consciousness bigger than "I." Seen this way, everything is sacred. I'm sure deep down inside, you know you will one day be able to cope with the pain, although this glimmering hint of an idea may seem far away. The big picture needs time to reveal itself, but holding this process sacred means being open to the idea that grief has come to teach you something. There is pain in bliss, but suffering is a choice. The purpose of experiencing pain is to elevate us. Obstacles enter our lives so that we may overcome them and grow from them. Pain is temporary. It is here to help us grow and move us forward in a collective evolution.

We don't have time for death until it smacks us in the face. Then it is all we can think about—but death has always been here. Most of us who understand the sacredness of life know death well. Death opens an invitation to the secret club that has always been in plain sight but that you were never before able to access. This is where the terms "behind the veil" and "other side" come from because when you experience death firsthand, the illusions are pulled out from under you, like a rug in a cartoon. Yes, death lifts the veil. And when the veil is removed, we revisit our beliefs on what happens after we die.

Death transforms energy into something new that is beyond one's earthly identity—beyond their name, gender, profession, and roles in life—and straight through to their purpose. Seeing this wholeness keeps us grounded in faith and deepens our connection to the spiritual world. The physical body dies, but the soul lives on. In many ways, the idea of the other side is the discovery of a lost world. Somehow the conversation of death and of the dying has been left behind in our Western world and is waiting to be remembered and honored. When pain comes through packaged as grief, there's no surprise that it may come as a shock to your nervous system and beyond. This is something our culture simply does not talk about, but it is something that is vitally important for us to understand as we move forward, both in this book and in our lives.

They May Be Gone, but Their Love Isn't

Although your loved one is gone physically, their spirit lives on, and so does their love. It is time to learn a new language—a language that can only be heard in silence and felt in your heart. Your passed loved one has not left you but is simply in the "other room," waiting for you to acknowledge them. They are ushering in help and love from a place of freedom and forgiveness.

Keep them nearby and feel their love by practicing silence, processing your emotions, and allowing yourself to heal. Emotions like anger, sadness, and guilt block our connection to the spiritual world. These emotions have a density that tugs at our soul. We must rise to meet our loved ones, and that comes from uplifting beliefs that unbind our minds and drop us into our hearts. Emotions like love, gratitude, joy, and serenity open our ability to vibrate at a higher frequency. Have you ever noticed that when you are really happy, people are attracted to you? When we take time to process dense emotions, they transform our bodies into higher states of consciousness. In these states, we are able to meet Spirit and communicate. Think of it like a walkie-talkie: We have to be on the same channel to communicate.

Your loved one may be showing you their love through different signs and symbols that catch your attention, which we'll discuss more later in the book. Trust these signs. When we lose someone we love, what we learned as children from our religion and/or culture may not fit what we are experiencing. You'll need to find your own truth in this reality. There's a misconception in some theological teachings that we need to surrender our power to something outside ourselves. The spiritual powers in the world do not exist only within chapel walls. Spiritual powers are within you.

I grew up in the Bible Belt of the South. Where I come from, churches are as common as Starbucks in Manhattan. In Bible study, we learned about God as a bearded white man sticking his head out of the clouds surrounded by angels. Something didn't make sense about this to me. The idea of being lifted into fluffy clouds and being invited through golden gates by a man holding a scroll never fit my vision of the afterlife.

Put this book down for a moment and close your eyes. Place one hand on your belly and your other hand on your heart. Take a deep breath in. Clear your mind. Relax. Imagine your version of "heaven." What do you see, feel, and touch? Whom are you with, and what are you doing? Sit with this image for a moment, and when you are ready, open your eyes and write down what you envisioned. Chances are you imagined people you love were with you. What fun is heaven if we can't be with people we love? Heaven is *here*, and we can speak to people who have crossed over. People may pass away, but their spirit and the love they feel for us never die. We all exist together.

When to get help: *One of the best paths you can take when the world is feeling heavy is to seek professional help. A professional mental health specialist is a wonderful resource to have in your tool kit. There is a difference between experiencing grief and depression. If you are having thoughts of suicide or self-harm or are feeling really low on energy, put down this book and contact a mental health specialist now.*

Sudden Loss

When the death of a loved one comes unexpectedly, you may feel as if someone pulled the rug out from under you, as described earlier. If the foundation of what you know breaks quickly, you may be in a state of shock for quite some time. When mourning a sudden death, your world will look drastically different from how it looked the day before. It's not uncommon to repeat or replay the surrounding events of the death in our heads and ask questions like *How can this be? Where did they go?*—like a child witnessing a bunny disappear in a magician's hat. (We all know the bunny is still there.)

The fear of further loss may also echo unconsciously in your emotions and habits. The ego needs a moment to catch up with reality. Like ripples from a big splash in a pond, loss can have a massive impact on your life that will take time to understand. Let your emotions settle before you make major decisions. Give yourself the courtesy of waiting until the water becomes clear.

Spirits from sudden passings often communicate to assure us here on Earth that transitioning to the other side is peaceful, no matter the circumstances. Pain is always described as temporary. No soul passes alone; all deaths are accompanied by assigned spirit guides to aid in the crossing over. Many spirits have reported that they subconsciously knew about their death while still on Earth and left signs and messages before the passing to remind their loved ones they are still here. For example, one man passed suddenly in an accident but had recently taken out a life insurance policy, to his wife's bewilderment.

His foresight supported his family as they mourned his tragic loss.

Expected Loss

Expected loss such as from a terminal illness or old age can be just as impactful as a sudden loss. Even when you know the time is near, it is difficult to fully prepare yourself for your loved one's transition. Regardless of how long you knew the time was coming, death still has a stinging aftereffect that takes time to settle into. The progress of processing the shock of death depends on our ability to find comfort in the uncomfortable—not in the timeline of transition. Even when a death is planned for financially and medically to the extent possible, nothing can prepare us for the difficult emotions of our fragile egos. Sharing memories and enjoyable moments with other loved ones is an enlightening way to celebrate a spirit's life.

Spirits often come through to communicate their gratitude to family members for their presence during the transition. Though they may have been unconscious, their spirit could still feel their loved ones' presence. I have communicated with enough spirits to know that the words and laughter communicated during transition are felt and heard. Although our loved ones may have suffered physical pain, all pain is alleviated when they return to their spirit body. When I see someone dancing, this is my symbol for a spirit who has had a long transition and wants to express to their loved ones that they are no longer in pain.

GRIEF MEDITATION

Sit or lie in a comfortable position. Take a deep breath in and place your left hand over your heart. Close your eyes.

Stretch your fingers out wide and feel the warmth of your hand over your heart. Ask that all shields or barriers around your heart be removed by Spirit.

Visualize your heart. See the tiny heart beating that conceptualized your life here on Earth. Recognize how sacred your heart is. Recognize how special you are.

As your unique heart beats, imagine a colorful ray of light moving across your heart. Imagine the ray of light healing any dark spaces or heavy areas in and around your heart.

Take a deep breath in, hold your breath, and count to 10. Experience the feeling of wholeness in your heart. Feel the presence of your passed loved ones lifting you up. Notice your heart feeling lighter.

Take another breath.

Now, be aware of all in your body that depends on the function of your heart. Know that you are able to return to this feeling of wholeness whenever grief becomes too much to bear.

Allowing Yourself to Grieve

Grief is stored energetically in our heart space. Symptoms of grief vary for different people. Some describe having a heavy heart or a perception that their heart is broken; you may also actually feel physical pain in your heart. In traditional Chinese medicine, the lungs symbolize grief, so you may also feel blockages in your lungs. Grief can manifest as emotions you can't control, unruly and unbalanced emotions, the inability to express what you are feeling, and maybe even making rash decisions. When we experience the death of a loved one, a shock wave of stress reverberates throughout our entire energetic system. While it can be uncomfortable, we need time to process grief. Connecting with Spirit is not here to replace the healing that must take place. When grief is not processed (that is, when it is buried away or ignored), physical ailments may manifest. An example of extended unprocessed grief is a hunched body, as if the person is trying to protect their heart.

Yes, this is an uncomfortable time, but there are a few things you can do to feel better while processing your grief. Try one or all of these:

1. Take a 10-minute walk in sunshine: Physical movement and vitamin D, which your body receives from sunshine, both boost your mood. Plus, being in nature eases intense emotions by grounding their charge in the earth and removes energetic blockages around the heart.

2. Turn on music and dance around your room: Cue: "Alexa, play some party tunes." Shaking your body for at least three minutes (about the length of a song) improves blood circulation and releases depressed energy stored in your body.

3. Give yourself the best bath of your life: Beforehand, place a little chocolate on your pillow or spray your sheets with a lavender-scented linen spray, like a fancy hotel turndown service. Then light candles, sprinkle flower petals in the bathwater, drop in a fancy bath bomb, and set an intention over the water to release difficult emotions. Afterward, put on a fluffy robe as you prepare for bed. This is a great way to release emotions and have an ugly cry. Wake up feeling refreshed, knowing that you have the power to hold yourself naked crying on the bathroom floor and can still greet a new day in the morning. This is called "release," and the ability to express your emotions with control is called "emotional intelligence."

4. Let yourself go: No matter how much we want to be on a certain healing timeline, we aren't in control. The truth is, healing looks different every single day. Sometimes you may need to binge-eat on the couch instead of working out. Screaming at the top of your lungs may feel better than meditating. The best gift you can give yourself is the gift of compassion. Let yourself regress when needed and try again another day.

CHAPTER 2

Healing from Loss

I woke up mourning my dog Jake (though he was still quite alive) the day my new client Rachel came in for a session. I was guided to lead her in a healing meditation to ground ourselves, and then we began. "Yes, I have a young man here who loved to race cars," I said. "He is showing himself passing in an accident, and it is not clear what happened yet. He wants you to know that he died peacefully and not to worry."

The feelings welling up through me were overwhelming. This spiritual connection told a story of authentic love and a turbulent romance. He had been a thrill seeker and a lover of the outdoors, and he had a special fondness for his beloved car. The most profound part of this session occurred in the last few moments. I wasn't mourning my dog Jake that morning. This was Spirit communicating with me prior to the session. Everything started to make sense. "His name is Jake," I said, and Rachel burst into tears and nodded. The opportunity to process my own feelings of mourning before seeing this client was an upgrade to my emotional intelligence, clearing the storm for this beautiful client. Mediumship is energetic work; energy healing happens in every session I sit in—for anyone around or in the session.

Like me and the clients I see, you are supported in more ways than you can ever comprehend. When I say you are not alone, I mean it in more ways than that just on the physical Earth plane. We are connected, and when we pass, a collective healing occurs. Our ego makes us feel as if we are all alone in our experiences. You may feel this loss has happened *to* you. This isn't the case. I invite you to consider the perspective of your higher self, that this loss has happened *for* you. No matter how tragic, the timing of someone's passing has reason.

Healing Doesn't Happen Overnight

There is a difference between experiencing grief and suf-fering. Choosing to process your emotions is you being in your power. Suffering is the suppression of these emo-tions and blaming it on something outside yourself. It is normal to be in shock and take some time to accept that your loved one is gone. It is what we make up around our experience with death that creates the suffering. However, we cannot fear suffering. Suffering is a part of life. The suffering and pain is small compared to the infinite power that you are. You are stronger than your circumstances. Although it may not feel like it right now, things will get better through time. This moment of death will teach you lessons along the way that will impact you in ways you may not understand in this moment.

Take your time in feeling better. Don't rush your process. Learn to embrace the unknown, the heartache, and the adventures that presume from them.

Take It One Day at a Time

Peace begins with acceptance. When you are ready, accept what happened and what is. Let go of any stories that you may have used to protect yourself from the hurt you feel. Be gentle with yourself. Our ego is loud and needs constant attention, while our soul seeks silence for comfort. The willingness to experience silence and stillness within our hearts gives us the ability to be present with ourselves.

Emotional stress can deplete the body, so remember that the way you respond emotionally is a choice. The accumulation of these emotional choices builds the foundation for your mental health.

Access silence with this grace, one day at a time. It is not about how you show up, but that you show up. In one of her podcasts, Oprah Winfrey said that the first question she asks during an interview is "How do you take care of yourself?" She mentioned that sometimes people actually cry because people have never even thought of this question for themselves. This question has a lot of merit, especially in the workplace.

Those who take care of themselves regardless of what is going on are aware that they have the choice to suffer or to manifest healing. A lot can happen in life that we put before ourselves, and the noise of everyday life often drowns out what we need. People are rarely comfortable in silence. Our lives have become so loud with TV, Netflix, smartphones, and so on. When is the last time you listened to silence? When is the last time you took care of yourself? If you were in an interview with Oprah, would you cry if she asked, "How do you take care of yourself?" The choice to take care of yourself is yours, but your soul wants to be held through this grieving process. We all want to know that we are loved, seen, and taken care of— this begins first by doing it for yourself.

In the spiritual world, healing is time. Time is marked through cycles and lessons. The spiritual side of life does not see time like we do, with watches and alarms. Time is not something we can control and manage throughout our day. Time is absolute. Time comes from the heart and lapses over into this very moment. Time is evolution.

Time is not linear, and neither is your grieving process. What can you do right now, today? Stop postponing your self-care, because this is where spiritual communication comes alive. Get to know your own love language, take yourself on a date, gift yourself a massage. Here is the permission you need splurge on yourself. It is time to experience radical self love. Ask yourself these questions and write them in your journal: Where can I slow down in my life? What would people's responses be if I slowed down? Where can I ask for help? What is the first thing that comes to mind when I think of my desires? How do I love me?

Your Feelings Are Always Valid

If there is anything you take from this book, I hope you gain permission to feel your feelings. I've seen clients, especially men, who have not cried in years. Suppressing our feelings creates *dis-ease* in the body, but when you release emotions, you actually raise your vibrational frequency and reprogram the trauma stored in your body.

Sometimes we may not feel safe expressing emotions we have been holding on to, especially if we haven't addressed them in many years. You may feel as if you will be stuck in your emotions, as if you will be mourning forever. The truth is that it is safe to give yourself time to feel your feelings. Being in the presence of these emotions is like riding a hurricane at the eye of the storm. This is where the peace lies.

Don't fear the storm; you *are* the storm. It's okay to walk yourself through the memories of the human life you are mourning and feel all the feelings they bring up. You may also have vivid dreams, which are not only common but also healthy and necessary. Dreaming is the first development of communicating with Spirit. The emotions you feel and the memories you experience will become symbols over time. These symbols cue communication from the afterlife. In other words, memories or thoughts of your loved one don't occur randomly; they were placed there by Spirit.

However, be mindful that unresolved trauma stored in your body may create disillusion. How can you tell the difference between trauma and Spirit speaking? Peter Levine, in his book *Waking the Tiger*, gives us some symptoms of trauma to look out for: hyperarousal, constriction, dissociation, and helplessness. If you feel those, they might not be signs from Spirit.

Your dearly departed is with you as you mourn. Emotion, grief, and the longing for their physical presence actually strengthen your spiritual communication with them. Feeling your emotions is one of the most powerful ways to grant yourself access to peace. Pain is never permanent. Imagine a pebble that drops into a calm lake: The water ripples, but soon enough the water becomes clear again. This authentic moment in your healing journey will come in different waves, but be willing to go through this emotional passage with pride in your ability to feel intense emotions and know that you will be okay, even when things aren't okay at the moment.

The Importance of Connection

This moment is meant to be shared. If you are feeling like this is only happening to you, get out of your element and share what's on your mind with a friend. You are not alone in your healing. There are amazing grief support groups and spiritual communities waiting to support you. I suggest therapy to all my clients who are mourning. There is no harm in setting up a time to talk with a professional. Sharing your story can also help others who may not be where you are; they may reflect back on what you said when they experience similar circumstances. Healing is collective: Your story is your story, but the lessons we learn from encounters with others shape our experience of the world.

Your "me time" is important, but so is socializing when you are mourning. Finding a good balance of letting people in and your "me time" depends on what you need, which may change throughout this journey. People who once supported you may not be the people you go to. Notice who is here for you and who isn't. Sometimes people may be uncomfortable around your grief, but this has nothing to do with you. You are reflecting back to them something they are suppressing or don't like about themselves. Death is one of the most visual times, where you see people's true colors and agendas. This does not mean people are wrong; they may simply have different intentions than you do. That is okay. You don't necessarily need to cut people out of your life, but maybe rearrange your "people list" so that it supports you. Ask yourself, "Whom do I feel most energized around? Whom do I feel most at home with? Who drains my energy?" These three questions can give your inner compass some clarity on how to establish boundaries and where to go from here.

The Ripple Effect of Grief

When you are mourning as a family or as a group of friends, things can get weird. It is just that simple. People act strange around death, especially if they have been suppressing emotions for years. You may find that people don't know what to say or how to talk about what happened. That's okay because you may be going through your own cycles of wanting to talk about it and not talking about it. So much can happen around death, and rarely is it peaceful. People will surprise you in the state of grief, so hold your own by defining what is okay and what is not. It is a good practice to assume that everyone has your highest good at heart, and if someone says something that makes feel you uncomfortable, request that they use a different phrase. The more you lead with gratitude and choose to see the good in people, the less you will mind what they say about the loss. Remember, people's words have little to do with you and more to do with their own experience.

Grieving with others is like adjusting your own oxygen mask before assisting others on an airplane. Take care of yourself first. Selfish is the new self-care. If you don't take care of yourself, you can't take care of anyone else, including children. When you are mourning in a family, finding some stability for yourself can help you support others. Friends or family who have suffered the same loss need compassion. To me, compassion is empathy in action. When we are able to facilitate a compassionate view of ourselves, we are also able to give that to the world. In this way, the ripple effect of grief can turn into the ripple effect of joy.

Acts of kindness are a great way to boost your mood. Something as simple as a smile or even bigger, like forgiveness, can have a huge impact. Being of service to another person actually makes you feel better and supports your mourning process. Try it today. Go out of your way to do something kind for another and see how you feel. Love has no words. It is not something we can do.

Love simply exists. An act of kindness is only impactful when your state of being is coming from love. We can *be* love, but we can't *do* it. There is a statement that goes "Be, Do, Have." When we focus on our state of being, the doing happens effortlessly, and then we have what we desire. This process makes doing tasks we don't enjoy come effortlessly, amplifying joy not only in our lives but also in the lives of those around us.

An act of kindness can be as simple as being in silence with another person who is also grieving the loss and being present with their words. Listen to listen, rather than thinking of how you will respond or comparing your own experience. Often, in shared grief, competition can arise. Our ego wants to create separation, but we all need each other—sometimes more than others. The best thing we can do is to truly listen to understand and, even better, repeat back what you heard them say. Look them in the eyes. Connect with that person and see yourself. Through this perspective, ask questions to more deeply understand yourself, the other person, and grief as a whole. Love the person, be patient, and give them permission to be themselves without opinion, advice, or comparison.

Moving Forward

How you move forward after loss depends on your current situation. Some people learn to cope quickly and start living a life without their loved one, but sometimes, mourning can take much longer. Change is the only thing in our lives that is consistent, and the sun will always shine tomorrow. Nevertheless, I have seen some clients who were living like it was Groundhog Day since the passing. For example, losing a child can be devastating, and I often find that clients are unable to clean out their departed child's room or space, even after a long time has passed. At times, you may hold on to more items that belonged to your loved one than you are physically capable of maintaining. The time will come when you are ready to move forward, and you will know this because you will feel an urge to clean out the space.

We know we are beginning to heal when we start having clarity about how to move forward. Silence becomes comfortable, and gratitude is accessible. We become more ourselves. I have watched many friends and clients heal throughout the years. When healing takes place, a weight is lifted. Metaphorically and physically, the emotional weight of trying to be something we are not is too heavy to carry. The weight of perpetual suffering and mourning has no use for you. We are here to shine our bright, beautiful lights. Healing takes place when we let go of what we think we need to be who we are.

It is okay to feel joy after losing someone close to you. Your life goes on, and the point in life is to be free. Let your life flow in the direction that is right for you. If something feels too hard, it may not be right for you at this time or at all. Take your time to heal your way and move forward with your life. There is no right way to do this. Let the pain and mourning serve you.

Your Experience Can Help Others

Your experience of grief can inspire others even if they have never lost someone close to them. It is safe to be vulnerable and share your experiences with others. Death brings people together and offers new perspectives on life. For example, one of my friends lost her full-term baby at birth. Her loss made a huge impact on our local area because she openly and bravely shared her experience on social media. She was a voice for women who'd had similar experiences. Her story created conversations around miscarriages and stillbirths, a subject that is often suffered in silence.

Speaking and sharing her situation uprooted other women's experiences that they had been suffering with in silence. Some even holding onto stories of miscarriages or the death of a child for years. Freeing yourself from pain by vocalizing it frees others, too. Shame and guilt keep us hidden in times of sorrow, but having the bravery to share your life in the ugly, raw moments makes the world a better place.

You never know who is listening and what impact you make simply by telling your story. Yes, the grief process looks different for everyone, and your story is special. But sharing it with others and listening to what others have been through can create a positive impact in our communities and the world.

CHAPTER 3

Keeping Your Loved Ones Present

One breezy fall day I had an appointment with a bride-to-be, Meghan, on her wedding day. Devastated by the loss of her father a year earlier and wishing for him to be near, she booked a session with me. That morning, I found her in a cloud of hairspray and wrapped in a silk robe. As the bridesmaids chatted, Meghan and I snuck away into another room.

I felt dizzy as the power of Spirit became more prominent. "I have your father here," I said with a sigh of relief. (I do not have choice regarding who comes through. Fortunately, the father–daughter bond between these two souls was strong.) "I wouldn't have missed this moment in a million years," her father shared, and then expressed his love for his daughter.

Meghan and I sat in brief silence taking in the beauty of the moment. Her father's tears poured through my eyes, and the bride and I both cried. Like any doting father on his daughter's wedding day, he shared stories of their time together, some of which were borderline embarrassing, and Meghan blushed. She savored each word with sacredness and attentiveness. She laughed when he shared the story about the red bicycle she'd learned to ride on. He talked about her first high-school dance and how nervous that night had made him. He spoke of each memory in detail to remind her he had always been there and would always be by her side. He evidently adored his daughter, approved of the groom, and was there to celebrate.

As we began to wrap up, he said, "I am here, and you will smell me." The bride nodded, deep in thought. "Smell me?" she murmured, to which I replied, "It feels like he means his cologne." Then she blurted out, "Can you tell me what cologne he wears? He wore the same one all his life. Can you tell me?" The connection closed as my anxiety and ego narrowed in, trying to get the correct answer. Her father's spirit interrupted my thoughts with this last remark: "I will not say, but tell her she will smell me."

A knock sounded at the door, and Meghan was swept into the whirl and twirls of a wedding day. It was a big affair at a swanky resort hotel. The bride looked stunning in her white gown against the sea of black tuxes and sparkly dresses. Meghan and her groom smiled all evening. Time went by quickly into the late-evening hours.

The next morning, I awoke to a text message: "I smelled him! You are not going to believe this!"

I have experienced some crazy synchronicities with spirit communication, so I trusted her. Her dad had spoken clearly, and I knew from his tone he would not disappoint. I replied, "Please tell me, tell me more."

Meghan texted, "So, after the reception, our friends convinced us to join them in their hotel room for after-hours drinks. We were not going to go but decided to surprise everyone last minute."

Me: "AND . . ."

She wrote back: "Well, I got to the hotel room, and my dad's cologne was sitting on the dresser. It was screaming my name. THE EXACT KIND!" She went on to explain that one of her friends had accidentally packed his cologne in his carry-on, and security had thrown it out. With only a few minutes before the wedding, he had run into a local pharmacy and grabbed the first cologne that smelled good to him, which happened to be her dad's cologne, which she recognized when she saw it. Although she thought it was weird when I told her she would smell him, she understood now. She had been smelling her father all night. He had hugged her before she walked down the aisle, she had danced with him, and she'd even had late-night drinks with him! She concluded her text with "Now I know he was there the whole time."

We all are like a bride on her wedding day all the time; there are many distractions and exciting things going on here that sometimes we do not hear (or smell!) our spirit friends. But they are *always* near and supporting us in this very moment. Spirits creatively weave themselves into our everyday lives in more ways than we can ever recognize. We are the ones who lose focus. However, when we are embodied, we are grounded; we know who we are and who we are not, which is important to understand when communicating with Spirit. The clarity and strength of the connection between us and passed loved ones depend on our ability to connect with the spirit inside ourselves. The only way is through our own spiritual connection.

Embracing Those Who Have Passed

Shiva is the Hindu deity responsible for the destruction of the universe. Interestingly, shiva is also the seven-day mourning period following the funeral of a loved one in Judaism. (These terms are spelled the same in English, but their names are independent.) The deity Shiva is known as the destroyer of the illusions in our mind and the limiting ways we see the world. When the illusions of our minds are pulled from us, we see the person who has died as a soul—no longer as a father, mother, husband, wife, son, daughter, and so on. Their roles in our lives become expansive as they shape-shift back into the spiritual bodies from which they came. Practices such as sitting shiva give us the opportunity to let go of the illusions we placed on the soul who has passed. The loved one you are mourning played many different roles in life. As you see them in their wholeness now, you can also keep their memory alive, which will help you on your mourning journey. This is the time for not only remembrance but also a life review.

Memories are the most important possessions anyone has. Take time to gather memories and surround yourself with others who have stories of your loved one. It is not the physical collections of things we acquire that are important. It is the details of shared experiences and the memories that keep the connection to the spirit alive. Mourning is a time to surround yourself with people who share love for this person's life. It is our ego, the illusion of our mind, that grips on to the material remembrances. Memories are what create symbols, which are the language of the universe and the spiritual world. We activate symbols by sitting in meditation, journaling, or lighting a candle in prayer. (You will learn more about signs and symbols later.) I guide clients to take nature walks after setting an intention to connect with their loved one and symbols on the trail. You can also go to a place of worship and pray. Some use a necklace or a piece of jewelry to hold in remembrance.

You can also take an action in honor of your loved one's memory. Volunteer at a local food bank, coat drive, or something pertaining to a passion of the person who has passed. Getting out of your comfort zone to help others enhances your communication with the spirit world. It is easier to notice signs and symbols when you are outside your normal routine.

During a session with a client named Sara, I was guided to bless a ring on her finger. Prior to this, we had been working on the success of her growing spiritual business for six weeks. I was communicating with her mother, who had informed me that Sara was wearing her mother's wedding band. Sara confirmed and agreed to bless the ring. She took it off her hand and held it in the palm of her hands. We prayed, "Angels, Masters, and Guides, please step forward now to activate this ring to support Sara at this time. May she feel the presence of her mother and know that she is guided and protected everywhere she goes. May she feel the power that she is and initiate it into action for her highest purpose." We then sat in silence and quietly held space to receive information from Sara's mother. Then we took a deep breath and looked each other in the eyes. With a nod, Sara placed the ring back on her hand. Two weeks later, she booked a new job working for one of the top tech-industry leaders, and her income tripled. As Sara did, allowing yourself to be guided toward your higher purpose by loved ones who are no longer with you can have positive effects in your life. Try it for yourself.

What's Left Behind

Holding on to your loved one's material possessions can support your spiritual connection or overwhelm it, so, above all else, be guided by the wisdom of your heart. For example, a client in her mid-20s came to me for a session. She had inherited her father's businesses and cars and had been trying to uphold his legacy. She came to me to seek her father's approval to sell the businesses. As soon as we began, I felt an intense pressure on my shoulders. As it turns out, he was more than happy for her to be free of the big responsibilities hanging over her. The physical presence of his businesses and cars was an illusion compared to what this man meant to his community. His legacy lives on through her, whether or not she is running his businesses. The lasting impact he made on this Earth was commemorated in much bigger ways than by holding on to something that was only meaningful while he'd been alive.

Yes, it is ideal to have practical details sorted out beforehand, but that's not always possible. Even then, sometimes we agree to something we cannot handle. It is okay to let things go. Go with the flow and listen to the spiritual guidance that is being offered to you. Activate your voice, make bold requests, and feel empowered in your decisions.

I have seen it all—from inherited donkeys and businesses to guitar collections and preserved bedrooms. Take the time you need to hold on to your loved one's possessions and mourn. For instance, I slept with my great-grandmother's bathrobe for a month after she passed. Doing something like this is nothing to feel shame over. It's normal to get creative with material items after someone has passed. My great-grandmother's bathrobe meant nothing to me until she was gone, but then I saw her bathrobe as the last scent of her on Earth. Other people may not understand what you need to do, but it's okay to allow yourself any moment or action that brings you closer to your loved one.

Be kind to yourself. Trust that your body will tell you when you are ready to let go of material items. When it comes time to decide what to keep, hold on to what you will use in your daily life. Guilt is a very low frequency. If you are holding on to something that you feel like you *should* keep, here is your sign: Let it go. Only you know what is true to your heart. It is best to think about how something will impact your life.

When my mom and I cleaned out my great-grandmother's five-bedroom house, there was so much stuff. We narrowed down the things we wanted to keep and what we were going to sell by simply asking each other, "How will I use this? Where will I use this?" If we couldn't think of an answer, we would sell or donate it. We made a pact to not keep items stored away but to integrate them into our lives. Still today, I have this weird pig-shaped porcelain creamer pitcher that has moved all over with me and is on display in my living room. It means nothing to anyone else, but for me, it reminds me of my great-grandmother's pantry, which she called the "cookie room." This pitcher is a portal into a different timeline.

Connecting with Your Loved One

There are myriad ways to communicate with passed loved ones, but there's only one way through: our hearts. When we begin to have a desire to listen to Spirit, we also dispose of the way we once saw the world. Spiritual beings do not have bodies and exist in higher frequencies; therefore, we must raise our frequency to meet theirs. This is the language of the heart. To raise our frequency, we must connect with our hearts and be present in our bodies. Sure, you can speak to your loved one out loud. You can also scream at the top of your lungs, but can you hear them? We, as a society, have been taught about prayer and asking, but most of us have not been taught how to receive. Meditation is a basic gateway into receiving and listening to messages from your loved one, including from your dreams.

Even if you do not dream, take a moment to listen when you are going to bed and waking from sleep. This is the most prominent time for alignment with your spirit body. There are many religious and spiritual beliefs around sunrise and sunset, as these are believed to be when the veil between worlds is the thinnest.

There is no wrong way to build a relationship with a passed loved one in the spiritual world. In the following chapters, we will take a closer look at different methods of communication, including journaling, meditating, listening to music, writing a letter, drawing, and stretching or doing yoga. Whatever method you choose, always set an intention for this connection. For example, you may say, "Angels, Masters, and Guides, support me now in the communication with [fill in the name]. Please only accept and give me information for my greatest good. Please send me clear messages that I can receive and understand."

CHAPTER 4

Communicating with Spirits

Katie came to a yoga session for a small group that I taught. In the silence of meditation, she felt the presence of her brother, who had recently passed away. After class, Katie admitted she had felt her brother since he passed. So much so, that one evening she took out her journal to document her experience. She was inspired in that moment to draw a unique flower. Although it was pretty, she didn't understand the full meaning until she spoke with her sister-in-law, with whom she felt called to share her experience. To her amazement, when Katie showed the flower she had drawn while feeling her brother's spirit with her, her sister-in law began to show emotions, because the flower that she drew looked just like white calla lilies. This was the last flower that he gave his wife before passing away.

Katie, eager to know why she felt him around her again, asked me, "Is this him? How was I able to know this? I feel there is more to be said."

This was his symbol to express a new way of living for Katie and her young family. She was here to light the way. She was a working mom who loved her job and her family. In this session we discovered she was a medium and the strength in her abilities was shared with her daughter. As she learned more about communicating with the afterlife, she was setting an example in the bond with her daughter. I also discovered through the spirit communication that there was much confusion over her brother's passing. As I picked up hints of his last living hours, I felt dizzy, foggy, and numb. I didn't know what was going on. I saw an open sky and felt anxiety about getting my shoes dirty. Then suddenly, *boom!* An impact occurred, but her brother showed no signs of pain. "Tell her I died in peace," he said, "I felt no pain. I was already high."

Communication begins with listening. This is an internal listening that, interestingly enough, uses no words at all. Yep, that's right: silence. Spirit communicates through nothingness. This is heart language—communicating not through our minds but through our hearts.

Understanding Spirit Energy

The first step in understanding human energy versus spirit energy is to recognize that you are a spirit. All the fluttery talk about lifting the veil is really about returning to your true nature, your spirit energy. You are a spirit first, and then you are human. To communicate with Spirit, you raise your vibration out of the dense body and move it into a higher frequency. You can do this by processing your heavy emotions like grief and transmuting them into lighter emotions like joy. Being able to face your heavy emotions or traumatic experiences helps you process what has happened and stay present to what is. The more we live in our truth, the more our frequency rises.

Keeping a high frequency can vary for some people, but the more you practice, the more you become stable in who you are. Instead of seeking ways to escape your present moment, find ways to be more embodied. When you are mourning a death that is especially uncomfortable, you may notice an urge to escape the present moment. That is why it is important to integrate small actions into your regular routine that keep you grounded in yourself. Of course, life wavers, but as you practice, you will get better at expressing joy rather than seeking it out. If you fall off the horse, just get back on. No. Big. Deal.

Here are six practices to integrate into your daily life to keep your frequency high:

1. **Be inspired:** Surround yourself with friends and family who inspire you and listen to you without judgment. You know who these people are because you will feel energized when you are or have been with them. Look for people who show up for you when you are thriving. Be careful around the friends who are only there for you when you are down.

2. **Keep growing:** As long as you stay focused on growth, your energy sparkles, and your spiritual communication will be clear. Don't know where to

grow next? Focus on what you love to do and do more of that.

3. **Meditate:** If you want to communicate with Spirit and accurately interpret messages, spend at least 10 minutes in meditation.

4. **Be in service:** Being in service can take you out of your misery and raise your vibration quickly. A random act of kindness, such as helping someone carry their groceries, can increase your awareness of the world around you and dissolve lower-minded thoughts. It gives you purpose. What is important about being in service is that you do something for someone without seeking anything in return.

5. **Live from the big-picture view:** When we see the wholeness of others and the world around us, we experience the wholeness within ourselves. For example, you are not sad; *sad* is simply the emotion you are experiencing in this moment. The sad feeling will change, and you will still remain. You are more than your emotions or the current situation. You are a being of infinite light.

6. **Sleep on it:** Sleep is not only how our body physically resets itself, but it is also how Spirit communicates with us. Documenting your dreams will help you stay on track with communicating with spirits. Studies show that even partial sleep deprivation hurts your mood.

The goal is to stay balanced in both your physical and spiritual body. The more rooted and grounded you are, the higher you can go. Opening communication with the afterlife supports us by strengthening our intuition. This can save us time because we can seek guidance from our loved ones for clearer decision-making.

When we open our access to the afterlife through daily practices, we come to the realization that we are never alone and this world is infinite. Our passed loved ones are eagerly waiting for us to communicate and ask them for support. Some ways we can communicate are to ask for guidance on a particular situation, to send healing prayers, or to ask to look over an opportunity. If you are passing through a hard time, you can ask for guidance on what steps to take to get out of it. First ask, and then sit back and listen for the message. The more you do this, the clearer you get and the easier it becomes. Remember, the question is more important than the answer. Spirit will respond to the exact question you ask. So be specific and direct.

GIFTS FROM OUR LOVED ONES

Messages from your passed loved one can come in physical form—really, a true gift from Spirit! Spirit can put things in our path to let us know our loved ones are with us. For example, a penny, feather, rainbow, name, number, animal, or person can show up in our path to let us know we are supported. The more you understand the symbology of the gifts that are presented to you, the more proficient your communication becomes. Studying the archetypes, the spiritual meanings of various animals, and researching common symbols that keep grabbing your attention help you do your part in strengthening your communication with Spirit. A simple Internet search will show you that there are many meanings to different symbols; the meaning you connect with the most is the most important one. (There's more on this in chapter 6.)

Making Contact

Guidance from Spirit is accessible to everyone who listens. It's a bit like singing. Everyone has the gift to sing, but some are naturally talented in this area. Some people may need to invest time into learning how to sing. The same works for the spiritual world. We all have a gift or an ability at varying levels. We also have different ways to communicate with the spiritual world, which means no two people receive messages from Spirit in exactly the same way.

With practice, you will discover what your strengths and challenges are in communication. No two people channel the same way. For example, you may be a visual communicator but looking for messages to be spoken to you through words. Your body has a unique energetic blueprint that is influenced by your DNA, your life experiences, the culture that surrounds you, and other reincarnations. Each person has every sense available for communication, but life experiences shape our communication style. For example, I work with a client who was raised by parents with a habit to reprimand her as a child by repeating, "You never listen." She took on the subconscious belief that she never listened, so the messages come, but she doesn't recognize them.

To open communication, discover what relaxes your nervous system and quiets your mind. This does not come from a forceful hushing of yourself, but certain practices such as getting a massage can calm you. This is considered self-care. To start communicating with your loved ones, you must learn how to relax. Overthinking will close down your lines of communication, so a good idea is to find time in your day to relax and be yourself. The following are a few practices that invite relaxation and strengthen communication.

Be Receptive

Your loved one is trying to connect with you. Their love for you gets stronger after death, even if there were unresolved feelings between you. Our passed loved ones see life from the bigger picture after death. It is up to you to be receptive to this connection. Emotional healing helps you see clearly and be more receptive. Feelings of anger, sadness, or guilt are dense emotions and bring down your frequency. To be receptive, face your fears and other feelings head-on and dissolve any feelings of mistrust of the world, yourself, and others.

Connect to Your Breath

Breath is life. When we breathe, we are able to calm ourselves and root into the present moment. When we are scared, our bodies tense up, and we hold our breath. This is a signal to our nervous system to either fight or run away. While a threatening situation may call for this, our bodies sometimes do this from conditioning, and this reaction may not always align with the truth of the situation. If we hold our breath and step into the fear, we only create illusions. However, when we are fully embodied by our breath, we relax our bodies and are able to trust what we are experiencing. So, the first step to communicating with the spirit world is to breathe. This will slow down your mind so that you can be embodied and see what *is* truth.

Meditate

Meditation is listening in silence. Quieting our mind relaxes and enhances particular parts of our brains that keep us calm, literally balancing our brain hemispheres and our emotions. This helps us organize the messages from Spirit. The most supportive meditation for connecting with the afterlife is learning how to "hold the power." This means opening yourself up to receive messages by making an intentional prayer and then allowing the energy to rise and expand within you; hold that power in place during meditation. (There's more on intentional prayers next.) You can start with 10 minutes and work your way up to an hour. There are many other types of meditations, too, including moving meditations, chanting, and listening to meditative music. Find a form of meditation that works for you and do it daily.

Pray

Meditation is listening, while prayer is asking. The answer we receive isn't so important, but the question we ask is. If we lived life in question instead of always seeking answers, we would all live in a much happier place. So, instead of asking, "What can I take?" try asking, "How can I serve with this connection?" Watch how your day unfolds differently.

I like to think of a prayer as if I am setting an intention. Interestingly, we pray all the time with the thoughts we think, and for many, this is unintentional. The words that course through our minds are like seeds we plant that grow into something bigger. Your loved ones are on the other side supporting you. If you continue to think, "I hate my job. I don't want to show up there anymore," don't be surprised if the path is suddenly cleared for you. That might not be what you intended. What prayers are you saying now? Are they uplifting you and taking you in the direction you want to go?

When we communicate with our loved ones, it is important to clearly declare what we are seeking. If the answer you receive doesn't seem aligned with what you want, go back to your question. Is there a way to be clearer with your message? Spirit will respond to *exactly* what you ask for. If you are not receiving what you intended and you feel your prayer is clear, check in with yourself to see if you are also saying unintentional prayers that don't support your higher vision.

It can help to have an opening prayer to use when you connect with the afterlife for clarity and consistency. Here is an example of an opening prayer I say before I connect: "Angels, Masters, and Guides, come through in this moment to use me as a vessel for Divine Spirit communication. We invoke through prayer that all messages that come through at this time be for the highest good of [*fill in the name*]. Please help me deliver them in kindness. All energies not here for this purpose, transmute into the light at your own free will or leave now." (You can use this opening prayer or come up with one that works better for you.) I conclude spirit communication by thanking all energies that came through. Then I envision light moving down my body through my feet until I feel that I am closed off from spiritual communication.

Set Intentions

Meditating and saying a prayer will help you set a target when communicating with Spirit, but setting your intention is how you hit the bull's-eye. You can be praying for one thing, but your intentions may be saying another. When communicating or asking for something, it is best to align your intention with your attention. You will not get the mansion you requested if you are not able to achieve the emotional and physical lessons that come with attaining that mansion. If your intention to communicate with Spirit is not pure, meaning that you have mixed intentions, your messages may not be clear. For example, if you want to speak with someone who has passed but are fearful of letting the divine into your life, the messages you receive may be vague.

When you have an intention that aligns with the highest good of all, you will receive messages at a quicker rate because your frequency is higher. This means that you are setting intentions that impact the greater good of the entire universe. To get yourself in that state of mind, ask Spirit this question: "What is in the best interest of the collective evolution?" Ask questions that get you into the awareness of your co-creation. You can ask your passed loved one for simpler things like "Where did I leave my car keys?" or "What are your feelings on me selling the house we lived in together?" These are also valid questions, but it is your "why" that will impact the answer.

Soften Your Mind

Your ego is your mind. It is really important to identify any lower-minded thoughts that keep you in a state of illusion. This can be a voice inside you that tells you that you are not enough, that you are making it up, or that you are a fraud. There is even a psychological term called "imposter syndrome" in which you may feel as if you are not what you say you are. Soften your mind around these ideas. Yes, in some cases, people have been persecuted for their spiritual or religious beliefs, so you are not crazy for having some fear around this, but you don't want the fear to overpower you to the point that you cannot access the gift to communicate with Spirit.

Belief in the afterlife is not new. Many tribal and primal communities from which we all originated had or have core values and rituals to celebrate communication with our ancestors. The beliefs of indigenous people have been suppressed. As a culture, we are still learning what impact this has had on our society. What's important to know is that you are more powerful than you think you are. When you get out of your own way, you step into possibility. Anything is possible when you believe in Spirit. Rid yourself of your ego's noises, and truly be free in knowing you are never alone and you are loved.

CALLING IN SPIRIT

To call in Spirit, begin by breathing to anchor yourself in the moment. Take a deep breath in, and as you breathe out, let everything go. Observe what you see around you without judgment. Just notice. Feel the air, feel your skin, feel the presence of others, and feel your breath.

When you are fully present, get quiet. Allow your mind to flow as it pleases for the first few minutes. Imagine that your mind is like a train station. As thoughts arrive, you have the choice to jump on the train, but you choose to remain in the station. If you get off track, no big deal. Come back to your breath. Come back to that station. Stay in one place; stay in your body.

Now that you have grounded your thoughts, access your heart. Feel the desires that are currently present— not other people's desires but your own true desire. What do you really want in this moment? As you align with your highest self, think and embody what it would feel like when you have what you desire. If this is spending time with a loved one, what would that feel like?

From this state of being, request the support of Spirit to move into action for your highest good and that all communication be clear. Clearly make a request to be seen and for evidence of spiritual presence in your life. You can keep your eyes open or closed. Here are a few opening prayers you may wish to use:

CONTINUED→

"I call upon all the Divine Power within me to empower my prayer of [fill in the blank] so that I may now feel, see, and hear proof of life after death. May I be energized and full of loving support for my highest good."

"Angels, Masters, and Guides, I call upon your support now in the communication with [fill in the blank]. Place around this connection a clear protection of light for the highest good of all. Please share clear messages and symbols that will empower my life for the highest good."

"I call on all divine powers of my highest good now to assist me in answering this question: [fill in the question]."

Relax and feel the presence of your passed loved ones working in your favor, supporting you, and showing you the love and guidance you need in this moment. If your loved one was still here on Earth, how would they answer this question? How would they want to be remembered? What was the character of the passed loved one? Did they have humor? Was this spirit more serious?

Let go of your need to overthink and allow yourself to receive. Stay relaxed and unattached to receiving a certain answer. Forget the question and allow what comes to come. Let Spirit surprise you by showing up when it is least expected.

Ask for Evidence

The best way to receive evidence of your passed loved one's presence is to ask for it. Evidence is proof that you are communicating with a certain spirit or with spirits in general. Evidence may come in physical form or through an experience of déjà vu in a flash of a memory, the appearance of an animal or someone who looks like your loved one, a phone call, or even a billboard advertisement. Evidence comes through synchronicity—when seemingly random things line up to get a message across.

When I first started communicating with my beloved great-grandmother in the afterlife, I saw roses. The first time it ever happened was right after her passing. As I relaxed into a warm morning bath, I felt her presence and then saw her silhouette in the doorway, and I knew it was her spirit coming through. I asked for proof that it was her. She pointed to the door and told me to go outside. A memory of us together in her rose garden came to mind. I instantly remembered how the stems felt in my fingertips as she handed over a freshly cut bouquet. This memory played out in my mind there in the bathtub, feeling so real that it provoked an emotional release: I cried.

After my bath, my dog was scratching at the door to go outside. So I put on clothes, opened the door, took a big step out, and got smacked in the face by a rosebush! It was a peculiar bush because it had grown there overnight. This was certainly enough evidence for me. That week, I saw more roses than I had ever seen in my life. I even met people named Rose, and I saw paintings of roses. I felt like a magnet for anything that had to do with roses. My great-grandmother wanted me to have faith that she was with me, and her message was convincing.

While your evidence may not be as obvious as the sudden appearance of a rosebush in your yard, it can come in many multifaceted layers that are obvious only to you. It is important to not take finding evidence too seriously. We often try to do the work for Spirit, but let your loved one have fun with you. Let yourself be surprised and have fun right along with them. When you let go of how or where the evidence is supposed to come through, that's when you will receive the clearest evidence of all. And when you find the evidence, document it by taking a picture, writing it in your journal, or telling a friend.

Slow Down and Connect

Speak to your loved ones who have passed as if they are still here and have just simply slipped into another room. There's no need to rush through what you want to say because they are always with you. Know that when you speak to your loved ones, they will hear you. Tell them about your day. Go on a walk with them and speak to them. When you feel pressure throughout your day, call upon them for support. When you need help making a decision, ask for clarity. There is an entire team of spiritual beings in the spiritual world supporting you, including your passed loved ones. Let the energy of the conversation flow, giving and receiving information the way you would normally converse. Instead of bombarding a spirit with questions or requests, ask one or two questions and wait for a reply before asking another.

Your loved one will take on the same characterization as they had here on Earth when you connect with them, so if they were shy, they will be shy communicating with you. A shier spirit may need a certain tone or approach to feel more comfortable. On the other hand, if the spirit is all over the place, they most likely were like that on Earth. Those loved ones also need a certain tone or approach and maybe some direct requests, such as "Take a seat." Each spirit has their own unique personality, so you get to listen and decide how best to communicate with them.

I have a client who comes to me often, and every time he comes, I see his three aunts. They run around the room, offering up pastries and making sure everyone is fed. It can be challenging to understand who's who, but I stop and pause. They also argue about who is going to go first. I access patience and compassion and ask that they all sit down so that I can see, feel, and hear them properly. This client gets a good laugh at this. This is enough evidence for him to know exactly whom I am speaking with. If his aunts came in orderly and calmly, he would be unable to believe the rest of the information offered.

Ask Them to Come Closer

When you first begin to communicate with passed loved ones, especially if you are more visually connected, you may see spirits or signs but only from a distance. If you are only seeing signs and symbols and not connecting to their meaning, invite your loved one to come closer so you can have clarity through emotions. We want to call them in closer to us so that the communication is not just seen but also felt. There is an incredible amount of wisdom in emotions. Opening yourself up to feel a passed loved one's emotions does not mean the feeling will be permanent. You are more powerful than any emotion that comes your way. The same way you can ask for them to come closer, you can also ask for them to take a step back. You call the shots.

One time I sat down with a client whose passed relative was so close to me, he was nearly sitting in my lap! As soon as the session began, I described to the client what I was feeling and then asked the spirit to take two steps back. (When a spirit is overexcited to speak to someone here on Earth, they may get so close that the sensations become too loud.) After the spirit took two steps back, I could see and feel things that wanted to be communicated more clearly.

Another client came to see me after the loss of his son to cancer. When I first asked the spirit how he passed, I felt so nauseated I thought I might hurl right there in the session. I immediately asked the young spirit to relieve the pressure on my body. I confirmed what I felt and shared my experience with his dad, who understood and received evidence from my physical response.

In another case, I had a session with a local yoga studio owner in her studio. I had a beautiful experience with her ex-partner, who started the session. Then her father came, and silence fell upon me. I asked the spirit to come closer because all I could see was his silhouette at the door. He replied that he didn't want to take off his shoes. (Shoes had to be removed before entering the area we were in.) I expressed that he was a spirit, so it would be fine for him to come in just as he was. This was all confirmation and evidence for this client because she knew her father as quite the formal businessman who generally wasn't one to get comfortable on a yoga studio floor.

Receive the Message

Your loved ones are constantly leaving messages for you throughout your day and even when you sit with Spirit. They did not come all this way to communicate with you just to tell you they are there. Your loved ones are giving you guidance. The way to receive the message is to get out of your own way. Sometimes the message may need a few moments to be fully understood because Spirit will often give us messages with many meanings.

Do not let your ego interfere with the message. This means that you want to make sure that you are listening to your own desires before you connect with Spirit. A message from your loved one will never make you feel inferior or provoke fear in you. When your loved one speaks, they speak only from love. Know that any true messages that come from Spirit will uplift you, make you feel inspired, or trigger you in a way that provokes healing. Truth is spoken quickly with very little time to explain. The messages are unique in every experience. Their soft ways of communicating exactly what we need in that particular moment are never repeated and, when received, never forgotten.

Preserve and Honor the Connection

If there is only one prayer you say today, let it be "Thank you." At some point during my spiritual journey, I stopped asking for things when I prayed and started saying "Thank you" instead. This changed my life in many positive ways. Whether or not you feel gratitude, your loved ones are always there serving you with humility. Gratitude allows us to experience joy and amplify our connections. Being grateful is the secret sauce to receiving what you want in life, especially messages and connection with Spirit. When your loved one communicates with you in whatever way they choose, remember to say "Thank you."

As a medium, when I close down my connection with a spirit, I visualize a light source above my crown that moves down my body, through my feet, and into the Earth. I use my intention and willpower to close off and visualize zipping up like a jacket. This returns me to the present on the earthly plane. When I am closed down, I still feel guidance and support, but I am not open to receiving messages from other spirits or for other people, as this can be exhausting if it is ongoing. As you develop your skills, you may experience some overload yourself. When you communicate with the afterlife, it is important to preserve and honor the connection. Saying "Thank you" and closing off honors you, the spirit, and the source, and strengthens your gifts. Designate an ending time before you connect with a passed loved one through one of the rituals shared in chapter 5.

ENERGETIC BOUNDARIES AND COMMON BLOCKAGES

Boundaries evolve as we evolve. Healers are people who are healing and want to continue to heal. The more you practice and experience connecting with Spirit, the more your abilities will evolve. The actual growth is defined by the boundaries you are able to set based on your worthiness. Often, spiritually sensitive people have come upon this gift after humbling life experiences. Know that this gift is worthy of protection and that you will only open up when you feel that it is right for you. Not everyone is ready for you to share these experiences with them. You also may not be ready to bear the answer to the question you are asking. This is where blockages show up. The beautiful aspect of this work is that what is for you will not pass you. The best way to overcome these types of blockages in your life is to focus on any emotional healing you have to do. It is also in your highest good to allow people to come to you and initiate these conversations. If you have a partner, relative, or friend who does not believe in this work, respect their beliefs and never push this information on anyone.

Sensing Loved Ones

Spirit communicates in a variety of ways through the seven main clair senses (the different ways we use our senses with Spirit): clairaudience (hearing), clairempathy (emotions), clairtangency (touch), clairsentience (presence), clairvoyance (sight), clairalience (smell), and clairgustance (taste). Each of these is explained on the next few pages. As you read, notice which sticks out the most for you. Which is your strongest? Which have you yet to experience? Just because you connect in a certain way now doesn't mean it will stay like that forever. Communication methods change all the time.

Hearing Them

Have you ever heard a creak in the floor or some other random noise in the house or maybe even a whisper in your ear? This is an example of the many ways Spirit can communicate through our sense of hearing. A person who has clairaudience will hear music, words, or sounds communicated by Spirit. A person with this ability may be a musician; in their creative process, they may receive hints and beats in their head before they create a tune.

One of my clients has been developing her spiritual gifts with me through one-on-one coaching. She has been learning to communicate with a spirit guide who was once living here on Earth as her uncle. We had been working hard to establish symbols she could recognize. In one of her assignments, she asked for a sign, and soon after, she heard the song "Greased Lightning." She didn't understand the message until her next coaching session when she was explaining it to me. Suddenly, the image and sound of the car scene in *Grease* played out in her head. "Aha, he loved cars!" she said. "That's why I heard the song." Now she understands that whenever she hears this song, her beloved uncle is supporting her.

Feeling Their Emotions

The gift of feeling another's emotions is called "clairempathy." We often don't value our emotions as much as we should. Emotions enable us to connect on a deeply healing level and receive strong wisdom from Spirit. When we take on a spirit's emotions, we are able to better understand their perspective and find compassion for who they are as a soul. Emotions have great depth of knowledge and act like the glue for symbols and personality in communication.

To use your emotions to communicate with the afterlife, study the source of the emotions and seek support from your friends who will freely share what they are processing emotionally. The more you are able to authentically feel which emotions are yours and which are not yours, the better you will be able to develop intelligence in your emotional connection with Spirit. This also includes creating boundaries around what you are willing to process.

A woman I was working with to develop her clairempathy told me of an experience she had while visiting with her family for Christmas. Her new brother-in-law was joining the family for the holiday experience for the first time. At around noon, she had an intense emotional outburst and could not figure out where it was coming from. The sadness she felt was overwhelming. Later that day, she learned that her brother-in-law's grandmother had passed away suddenly at noon that day. He'd been holding in the news and his emotions, not wanting to ruin Christmas for everyone. My client was able to quickly articulate that this was the grandmother's emotion coming through; she wanted her grandson to know that she was still with him and loved him very much. When my client recognized this, she was able to separate her emotions from the experience and create more boundaries around the spirit and her brother-in-law's feelings.

Feeling Their Touch

Physically connecting with Spirit is called "clairtangency." This may feel like someone has touched you, but no person or object could have been the cause. Often, our passed loved ones are eager to reach out and give us a hug or hold our hand to show us love. Feeling a spirit's touch is not limited to a physical sensation; it can also come in the form of moving objects or knocking on walls. We can also use this ability while writing or journaling. We can surrender the pen and allow Spirit to move it across the page.

I was due to go on a business trip and was packed and ready to leave when suddenly I couldn't find my ID or credit card. I never took them out of my wallet, so I was baffled. I knew that this must be a passed loved one protecting me from something I didn't understand yet.

Despite my search, I missed my flight and then canceled the trip entirely because something told me Spirit had moved my cards for a reason. Nearly an hour later, a family friend had an emergency. I dropped everything to be there for her. The next day, guess where I found my ID and credit card? In my wallet. I am so grateful that I listened to Spirit's message and was able to be there for my friend.

Feeling Their Presence

When we feel the presence of a spirit through clairsentience, we may actually experience what the spirit would have embodied here on Earth. For example, if the loved one passed away from a stroke, you may feel half of your body become numb. If the spirit coming through was an active outdoorsman, you may feel an urge to shower. When we feel the presence of a spirit, we are opening up our bodies to experience them from a gut-like sensation. Have you ever felt a gut feeling? It may be hard to describe, but you know something for sure because of this feeling. This is how feeling their presence feels. As we develop this gut feeling, we can even distinguish gender, age, height, or personality traits. As they say, always trust your gut.

Clairsentience is a common way for healers and health practitioners to experience Spirit. A friend and fellow medium who has invested much time studying Reiki and other healing modalities feels when Spirit connects with her. One day, after dinner at her house, we sat on her balcony and opened for Spirit to come in. I said, "I see a man

with a beard." When I turned to look at her, she was strok-
ing an imaginary beard without even realizing it!

Seeing Them

Seeing spirits is called "clairvoyance," which can occur in
a couple different ways. Spirits may come in like an illusion as if they were still alive or physically in the room.
The second way is through a daydream. Have you ever
dreamed with your eyes open? This movie-like image
playing in your head is one way Spirit communicates.

Our passed loved ones will often use symbols to communicate a message. Some symbols can come through as
physical things, like a license plate, numbers on a clock,
or an animal. The symbols can also come through in our
minds. Moreover, you may see an imprint or a flash of
color in the darkness of your closed eyelids. In the presence of Spirit, I often experience flashes of light while my
eyes are open. This light is quick and can be mistaken
for lightning.

With clairvoyance, you may also have the psychic
skill to see auras on a person here on Earth. Auras are the
dancing rainbow of colors that can be seen or felt around
our bodies. An aura can look strikingly similar to the state
of our immune system. Have you ever seen Pig-Pen in
the *Peanuts* cartoons? That is you, walking around in a
cloud full of energy and germs. Spirits have auras, too,
since they have energetic bodies, and that is where auras
exist. People who have the ability to interpret auras can
benefit from having a pen in hand when communicating
with spirits. Better yet, bring out markers, chalk, or paints,

because the more you can express colors, the better you will understand an aura. Let your intuition guide you on what colors to choose and see how you interpret a spirit's aura.

I went to get a massage one day, but instead of going to my usual place, Spirit guided me to a specific massage place near my house. I was greeted by the massage therapist and brought into a room to change. As soon as he closed the doors, I saw a big flash of light in the dimly lit massage room. I knew it was his passed grandmother coming through. I kindly asked him before the massage if I could share some of the information I was receiving. He happily accepted. I saw his grandmother in beautiful gowns dancing onstage in such a marvelous way. With permission, I shared what was being communicated through me. The therapist confirmed that his grandmother had been a professional salsa dancer. Her favorite moments of her life were dancing onstage in Cuba. He was grateful for the message, and I was grateful for the wonderful massage.

SPIRIT ORBS

Spirit orbs are a collection of floating lights seen in a photograph or experienced in person. These can appear as round dots of any color; they may actually create shapes, too. Clients often send me their "orb photos" after a session in which they connected with their passed loved ones. Perhaps you have seen orbs in your own photographs. These represent your passed loved ones, and they may have messages for you or just want to let you know they are with you.

One day, a friend who lost her baby at birth reached out to me because she felt emotionally overwhelmed around the idea of having another child. She was concerned that after the trauma she would not be able to get pregnant again. She really wanted to have another child but felt very scared. As we spoke over the phone, the camera on my phone randomly turned on. I saw three orbs coming through the lens. The first orb was clear and developed. This orb represented her three-year-old daughter here on Earth. The second orb was fading a bit, and it felt like her son who had passed at birth. The third orb looked faint, as if it were still developing. I knew this to be her child who had yet to be born. I shared this with her, and she was able to relax around her fear. A few months later, she found out she was pregnant, and within nine months, she delivered a healthy baby.

Smelling Their Scent

"Clairalience" is when Spirit sends us smells to trigger certain memories or thoughts of a particular person. This can be things like cigarette smoke, perfume/cologne, popcorn, or flowers. When you have the gift of clairalience, you may be sensitive around strong odors. This is a gift that shouldn't be taken lightly because great information comes through smell. Have you ever experienced the powers of a dog's sense of smell? We have that ability, too, if we practice it.

One day I showed up 40 minutes late to a pottery class I was taking. To my surprise, no one was there. *How can this be?* I wondered. Then, from down the hallway, I heard the instructor, Clarisse, say, "Hey, so weird no one showed up today." I approached her with an expression of confusion. The class had a dozen *devoted* students in it. Suddenly, I was overcome by the fragrance of petunias. There, holding the flowers, was an older woman. "I smell petunias so strong right now and see the spirit body of an older woman," I said. "Did someone pass?" Then I felt the presence of a grandma. "Clarisse, did your grandmother pass?"

The situation started to unravel and make sense. Her grandmother *had* just passed, and petunias had been her favorite flowers. Because Clarisse knew I was a medium, she had been praying to her grandma to use me as a vessel that day in her class. Her grandmother did this through the gift of smell and had somehow intervened so that Clarisse and I could have private time together that day.

Taste

When someone has a taste in their mouth that is not relevant to anything they ate or had in their mouth, it is called "clairgustance." Communicating with Spirit through taste often happens for people who work with food, such as chefs. It can also happen when you are cooking at home. The taste may trigger memories, or you may intuitively know which ingredient to add to a dish. Have you ever cooked or baked using your intuition and created something incredibly delicious? You may have been guided by your passed loved one.

My passed great-grandmother helps me bake all the time. I love to bake her special cookies and often look at the process of making them as a form of meditation. I don't need a recipe because she knows it by heart and directs me through clairgustance.

Dreams

It is common to see passed loved ones in your dreams. They may appear through symbols, a general presence, or the way you knew them on Earth. To properly understand your dreams, spend some time freewriting in your journal about what you think your dreams mean right after you wake up while they are still fresh. You can also ask a question you would like answered before you fall asleep. Write it down so that you can look at it in the morning and recall what happened in your dreams that may be the answer you are seeking.

Spirit communicates through different types of dreams: lucid dreams, daydreams, false awakenings, and nightmares. Lucid dreaming is when you are aware that you are dreaming. For example, I had a dream I was being kidnapped. I knew I was dreaming, so I made the choice to start the dream over. This time I made a different decision that led me to a dinner party with friends. Much more satisfying than being unconsciously kidnapped, wouldn't you say?

A daydream is communication that occurs when we are awake and can be typically described as "zoning out." A false awakening is when you wake up in the dream, but you are actually still sleeping. A nightmare is an uncomfortable dream that triggers emotions. All of these different types of dreams can provide you with important information if you take time to understand their meanings.

Here are a few examples of general messages Spirit may be giving you in your dreams:

→ **Baby:** New project, new beginnings, birthing new ideas

→ **Being naked:** Vulnerability, innocence, a reveal

→ **Flying:** New heights, freedom, new perspective

→ **Meeting a celebrity:** Fame, success

→ **Ocean:** Expansive, emotions, feminine, adaptability, flow

→ **Teeth falling out:** A big change, fear of being humiliated, new beginnings

→ **Tree:** Stability, family, roots

→ **Washing machine:** Cycles, cleansing, purify

→ **Water:** Emotions, intuition, cleanse

In chapter 6, you will find an A-to-Z listing of other common symbols. Whether you are dreaming or awake, the various signs and symbols you encounter hold similar messages from Spirit. Make it a daily practice to read about the potential meanings of various symbols in this book and from other sources to support your ability to interpret the messages your passed loved one sends your way.

CHAPTER 5

Rituals for Remembering and Reaching Out

When I truly remembered my spiritual gifts in this lifetime as an adult, I was on a yoga mat, mourning the unexpected loss of my little brother, just a year after my great-grandmother's passing. Recently cloaked in death, when I sat in meditation that day, the world suddenly made sense to me. After that experience, I would sense my brother during class and was able to communicate with other spirits who were there as well. One day in class, I put my mat down next to an older woman, Mimi. I had seen her in classes but had never really spoken to her. During the final meditation, I saw an array of colors and lights dancing around me when I closed my eyes. The different colors transformed into two silhouettes, a fatherly, older man and a woman who looked strikingly like Mimi.

The woman whispered in my ear, "We are Mimi's parents." The man came forward, opening the palm of his hand and wrapping his hand around Mimi's mother's. They both took two steps back, and I was able to see their full bodies. The woman spoke again, but she spoke for both of them: "Please tell her we are here together and we love her." After she spoke, I saw Valentine's Day hearts pour from their hearts into Mimi's, who was still lying next to me in meditation. Then the man walked over with a birthday cake and blew out a single candle.

"Come back to your breath," the yoga instructor said, closing this vision in perfect time. We wrapped up class, buzzing from our yoga high. I turned to Mimi and asked if she would mind if I shared the message I'd received for her in meditation. I told her about the vision and repeated everything, being careful to not leave out any details. Mimi looked attentive, but just when I thought that maybe I had said too much, a single tear fell from her eye. Soon, she began to cry. I could sense Mimi's warm demeanor and her ability to make anyone feel better when she smiled at them. Now she was being seen in love the same way she gave love to everyone around her.

A moment later, Mimi said, "In meditation, I asked for my parents to show me a sign that they were around. I didn't have a good relationship with them. They died at different times, and I was wondering if they are together and if they still love me."

I replied, "They do, Mimi. They love you very much and are together. Your father showed me that he has a birthday coming soon, and it must be around Valentine's Day. Does that have significance to you?" Mimi confirmed that her father's birthday landed on Valentine's Day, which was just a week away. It was the reason she had been thinking of her parents.

Meditation quiets our minds so that we can articulate what is coming from our thoughts, our heart, and Spirit. When we show up for our own gifts and for our own mental health, spirits will show up for us. If you want to speak to the afterlife, you must first learn how to speak to yourself. You can do this by creating rituals in your daily life that inspire you, excite you, and help you break out of your mind and drop into your heart.

What Are Rituals?

Rituals are daily meditative practices that cut through biased illusions, unconscious beliefs, and anything else distracting us from the relationship with our highest self. They place us in a deep, concentrated state that brings us back to ourselves.

The smallest part of your day can be a ritual, and it can have more impact on your life than anything else that day. This may be as simple as showing up to a yoga class. Rituals are meant to be flexible and adaptable, just like a yogi. Some examples of rituals include chanting mantras, exercise, being in nature, sitting in meditation, applying scents to your body, lighting a candle, spending time with someone you love, being in silence, and singing a song. Whatever the particulars are, rituals are performed to raise the frequency of your energetic state. This makes it possible to communicate with your passed loved ones. Remember to befriend silence to receive the answers.

As you open up to communication with the spiritual world and explore new rituals, there are a few things to keep in mind. Discipline, or devotion to a ritual, opens the door to freedom. Think of squirrels who are so devoted to their work and enjoy every moment. They are not sad and droopy about gathering nuts. They are playful, jumping joyfully from tree to tree. So we should be. In the Hindu culture, the deity Hanuman is a representation of devotion. He is always pictured as a playful monkey. Devotion is meant to uplift our lives in the moment, not tomorrow. These are tools to refine your physical body and attune to the divine frequency of Spirit. These practices enhance your present moment.

Listen and adapt to what your body needs in each moment as you mourn. This will change with every day, with any season, so see the light and go with it. Rituals tend to evolve, so what worked for you last year might not feel the same this year. Choose what excites you because that is the life worth living for. Be adaptable and don't forget to have fun. Rituals are meant to be repetitive. They are not about how you show up but that you show up. I suggest creating some rituals to do once a day for a period of time so that you can embody these practices as you mourn. Try committing for 30 or 90 days—give yourself a challenge. The more you show up for your rituals, the better you will get at speaking with Spirit. These rituals will also help you in your mourning process and boost your mental health.

You can incorporate anything into a ritual to open or strengthen your communication with Spirit. It is the intention behind each action you take that matters most. If we set the tone for that activity to bring in a loved one with an invocation, a chant, or a visualization exercise, that will completely change the experience. The most powerful times to connect spiritually are at sunrise and sunset. Later in this chapter, you will find a number of rituals with invocations that I personally use and share with clients to ease the mourning process.

SIDE EFFECTS OF SPIRIT COMMUNICATION

Spiritual beings may communicate through physical symptoms that will "upgrade" your body for you. Next time you fall ill, remind yourself that this is a spiritual gift and ask how it is meant to support you. Symptoms like ear ringing, fatigue, and headaches may occur if you are trying to do more than your share of work in connection. This is like hijacking the plane from the pilot and taking yourself off course. Let Spirit come to you.

To stay in your power, keep your focus turned inward. When we lose our personal power, symptoms show up in our body as pain. You may experience bloating, for example. This is the feminine aspect of carrying the weight because it mimics pregnancy and can actually affect a person's menstrual cycle. Other symptoms may start with being with someone else's thoughts (i.e., sharing their thoughts and finishing their sentences) or taking things personally, which can lead to stress, dehydration, and feeling fatigued. The more you listen, the more you realize you are given many hints. Listen to the signs. If you feel you have gone off course, you probably have. Spirits come through to let you know they have your back. They want you to know that, yes, they are there for all the moments of celebration and hardships. It is not for you to seek them out but to feel their presence in your heart. Trust and give the work away to the universe to support you.

Tools for Connecting with Spirit

There are many tools and resources you can use to remember your loved one, ease your mourning process, and connect with Spirit. These items support your experience. However, you are the strength, the soul, and the spiritual power. Remember when using tools to not give your power away to the tool. It is not the tool that draws Spirit in. It is you, and it has been in you this whole time. The tool is there to support the process.

Use what you have around you if you don't have the exact tool you need. However, the items you need may "magically" appear in your life as gifts from Spirit. You could find them, or someone may give them to you. In fact, the more you sit back and allow things to come to you, the more powerful your ritual will be.

An Altar

I suggest creating an altar to be a sanctuary for healing and communication to Spirit as you mourn. This a place with your own energy. It doesn't need to be massive; a little closet or corner will do. There are many types of altars, including a community altar for family or for a household, which is a great idea if everyone is mourning together.

When you bow to an altar, it is a sign of reverence for your current experience of your life. As you bow, you are metaphorically balancing the sky and earth, since as you bow you are becoming parallel with both planes. The deities or images that adorn your altar are meant to be reflections of attributes of your character that you want to feel. Your passed loved ones will use archetypes or spiritual teachers whom you follow to support your communication with them. Let what is meant to be on your altar show up for you. A healing stone, a coin, a photo of your passed loved one, a sculpture of an animal, a deity, a religious figure, or a piece of jewelry—anything can be held sacred in this space.

Let your altar build itself. When you create an altar, think of yourself as a bird gathering twigs and branches to make a nest. You are like a gatherer, and the things intended for your altar will appear to you. Sometimes we need to be humbled by bowing to an altar with nothing on it. Create the space and trust that what you need will be revealed to you.

There are a few energetic housekeeping tips on keeping your altar at a high vibration: First, keep this space clean and decluttered. Keep it off the ground and cover the space with a scarf or tapestry so the objects do not touch the surface. You never want to place these objects on the ground without something separating them from the floor.

Keep your altar facing east, the direction of the sunrise. Another option is to keep it facing north, which represents wisdom. Place something to represent each of the four elements to empower this space. For ether or air, you can use incense to honor the communication of your spiritual body. Add a candle here to honor the fire element, which represents discipline and passion for life. Use sacred water or forage water from the ocean or river or collect rainwater; water represents your emotions and fluidity in life. (I suggest changing this water daily.) An earth element such as healing stones, metals, fresh flowers, or soil grounds the space. Spending time around your altar will enhance this space in a special way. It gives you a designated place to mourn and to practice true spiritual connection with your passed love one.

Candles

There are four common candles to know about for a ceremony: pillar candles, tapers, votives, and tea lights. Pillar candles are molded with wax to stand alone. These candles are suggested for wax readings because they easily take shape as they burn. Taper candles or dinner candles are long, thin candles that need a candlestick or candelabra. These candles also are a good choice when it comes to receiving information through candle drippings. Votive candles can come in many different shapes and typically have some protective layer around them. These candles are suggested for use in reading smudges and wax spots. Tea lights are often used in ceremonies and can fit in small holders and figurines for your altar.

Food Offering

One of the oldest rituals to connect with our ancestors is offering food that we eat. This practice dates back to the time of the Egyptians and is still practiced in many cultures today. Buddhists, Christians, Hindus, and other religious cultures have practices where they offer food to Spirit. This practice welcomes and opens up spirit communication. Prepare the food on a clean, special dish. Leave it on your front doorstep to welcome your ancestors in or make a designated space on your altar. Offering food is an expression of gratitude or in case they get hungry, as described by Buddhists.

Make sure to change the food daily, as you won't want to attract insects. Take your time and make it meaningful. Keep this space held in high regard. Set the intention by speaking aloud to your ancestors as you prepare. Offer food by singing a song or light a candle. Part of your meal or simple fruits and nuts will do. Giving to spirits in this way symbolizes the abundance that we have in our lives and deep honor we show to the spirits who protect us.

Cedar

Cedar is a type of wood that has cleansing properties that call in your ancestors in a very grounding energy. It is associated with prayer, healing, and protection from diseases. In the Bible, cedar is a symbol of Mary, and the cedar tree is mentioned several times.

To activate these properties, bring the wood into your home and place it on your altar or burn it. Call in your loved one by breaking down the cedar to small bits that you can burn and use the smoke to cleanse your altar. Any heavy feelings or emotions can be cleansed by using cedar. Set an intention and move the cedar to the areas of your body or home that need healing.

Meditation Beads

Meditation beads have been used for ages to connect with Spirit. The most common are the mala, rosary, and mantra bracelet. Rosary beads are used in the Catholic faith to connect to Mother Mary, the divine feminine. The rosary evolved from the mala commonly used by Hindus, Buddhists, and Yoga vedandic traditions. Both are used during meditation and for getting connected with the spiritual world. Use what feels comfortable to you.

Meditation beads are made out of different woods, healing stones, and/or seeds. Each mala has 108 beads, which is a sacred number representing completion in yoga. When using mala beads, different Sanskrit mantras can be chanted to activate different purposes. *Japa* is Sanskrit for the repetition of a mantra. You can use a japa to activate emotional healing within you. Try the mala bead ritual on page 91. You can research other mantras if this is a practice you would like to continue.

Crystals

Crystal healing is a modality for healing your body and amplifying spiritual communication. Crystals have a molecular makeup that stores and amplifies energy. Different crystals do different things—for example, amethyst is a purple crystal with healing properties that can increase your intuition, while carnelian, an orange crystal, is a great stone to work with when you are looking for motivation. Crystals can be placed on your body in a crystal grid, worn throughout the day, or added to your altar or home to create the frequency you want in your life and to ease mourning. You can even put some kinds of crystals in your bathwater. Plants love the vibration of crystals, and you can place them in the soil.

Spirits will draw certain crystals to you; they also will lose or break crystals when your time with them is done. Bury any broken stones back in the earth, and avoid having broken crystals in your home. Many professional mediums and light workers hold crystals as they work to enhance the spiritual energy exchange. Suggested stones to work with as you grieve are angelite, rhodochrosite, and pink opal. Angelite aids in the expression of grief and the connection to the spirit realm. Rhodochrosite is a healing stone that releases sadness and balances emotions. The pink opal is a stone that softens and creates a nurturing feeling as you mourn.

Pendulum

A pendulum is a stone or medal with a fixed point that is held by a small chain. Its movement gives you answers to questions you ask of Spirit. A pendulum is used by holding the top chain in your fingers lightly in your left hand (your receiving hand in ceremonies) and hovering the pendulum away from your body. Your wrist should be relaxed, and care should be taken not to move the pendulum; it will swing on its own.

You get to create your own meaning for each movement, but here's how I interpret it: Right to left means no, and forward and backward (toward you and away from you) means yes. When it goes around in a circle, this signifies that there is no answer. You can use a pendulum while pulling oracle cards or asking yes-or-no questions. You can also draw out a grid with numbers or letters, or an either-or question and hold the pendulum above it.

Your Body

Your body is the most important tool from this entire list. Sweating once a day not only adds value to your actual physical health but also improves your spiritual and emotional body, too. There are so many different ways to exercise, so I encourage you to work out with your intuition. Do what you feel called to do. Maybe that feels like walking in a park one day and on another showing up for a boot-camp experience. Being flexible in your body means being flexible first in your life. Ask Spirit, "What activity can I do today?" When we create rhythmic movement, this is considered a moving meditation, and it will help you communicate with the spiritual world because it enlightens your spiritual body. While moving your body, breathe with intention.

Rituals for Connecting with Spirit

In this section, you will find a number of rituals to choose from. You can incorporate as many of these as you would like, mix and match them, or focus on just one. Do whatever feels good to you. Rituals are a part of nature, just as the leaves fall in autumn. You can adapt the rituals to support your evolution. One thing I have learned is that anything is possible when connecting to Spirit. You can use these exercises to not only communicate with your passed loved ones but also boost your mood. These are empowering life rituals that have the ability to change your life for your highest good. The more you do them, the better you will get at understanding the signs from Spirit.

Candle Ritual for Spirit Communication

You will need:

A candle (encased in glass or a taper in an appropriate holder)

A pen or permanent marker

A lighter or matches

Candle safety: *Never leave the candle unattended or place paper on the candle or near it. Be sure to set the candle on a fireproof surface as you let it burn.*

Decorate the candle by writing on the glass (or carving in the wax). Write the name of your passed loved one or a word you want to embody. Create an altar around the candle. Place a photo or something physical of your passed loved one around it.

To light, first hold the candle over your heart to charge it with the intention you have set. Close your eyes and envision a white sparkly veil of light being lifted from in front of you. As it is pulled away, envision your loved one standing in front of you on the other side with their hands placed over yours.

Sit in this energy and say aloud, "I call upon the divine force of the ultimate creator to empower my communication with [*insert name*]. Through this prayer, I invoke clear messages for my highest good. Anything blocking this communication or my divine purpose, fall away now."

Open your eyes and set the candle down or in its holder. Light the candle fully in this energy. As the candle burns, watch how the wax moves or how the glass smudges on the sides.

Your passed loved one will leave messages as the candle burns. Watch how the wax moves, how the wick burns, or if there are smudges on the glass. After the candle burns, see if you can make out any symbols from the wax or soot on the glass. Notice if you can make out animals or different shapes within the candle wax or glass.

When you feel complete, blow out the candle, trusting that your intention has been set and you will receive messages throughout your day or night. I suggest repeating this ritual for 30 days or throughout your mourning process. Do this in memory of your passed loved one and to empower your mourning process. You can use the same candle again and again for this ritual until it is completely burned out, or you can use a smaller candle that will burn out in one sitting. Never blow out a small candle.

You can also do this same candle ritual with a different invocation. This message is here to support you in your healing journey. Here are some alternatives:

- **For healing:** Say aloud, "I call upon the divine power to protect me in my healing process and upgrade my body now so that I am able to fully express the life that I am. Clear any illusions and place me in my truth now."

- **For empowerment:** Say aloud, "From all the divine wisdom and power invested in me, I invoke this prayer to free me from any constraints that bind me away from my highest self. I speak my truth in my power. It is safe to be me. It is safe to be powerful. I am free."

- **For purpose:** Say aloud, "I call upon all divine energy to align me with my highest purpose now. Reveal to me how I may be of service to this world. I am valuable and see my worth from this place I create."

- **For balance:** Say aloud, "Father Sky and Mother Earth, balance my emotional, physical, and spiritual body. I root myself in mother nurturing and link my belief system with the higher vision of the father. I am the perfect harmony of both energies. I am divine love."

There are many different signs that come from the burning of a candle, within the burning process and the aftermath when the candle burns all the way out. These are a few messages I've heard from passed loved ones through my own experience and with clients:

- **Black soot:** If you are burning a candle in a glass and the candle is covered in black ash, this is a sign that unprocessed emotions are blocking this communication. Try using the healing prayer to remove blockages and burn the candle again. If the candle burns clear, you know the message has now been received. Messages in the pattern of the black soot may be revealed. See what your imagination creates from the patterns.

- **It won't light or stay lit:** Check in with your intention. This may be Spirit's way of protecting you. Are you reaching out in desperation, or is this truly for your highest good?

- **Twin flames:** This represents connection to another person.

- **Popping flame:** A passed loved one is attempting to communicate with you. Your messages are heard.

The colors you see in the flames (or the color candle you choose) also have meaning. These colors are associated with the chakra system (the energy centers of the body).

- **Red:** Stay grounded. You are safe and secure.
- **Orange:** Your loved one surrounds you and is connected to you.
- **Yellow:** Your personal willpower is important now. Direct your focus on what you want.
- **Green:** Love is always the answer.
- **Blue:** Communication is important. Speak the truth and let your voice be heard.
- **Purple:** Divine wisdom is being given to you now.
- **Violet:** You are connected. Trust it.

Ritual to Offer Food to a Passed Loved One

You will need:

Freshly cooked food, nuts, or berries

A special small serving dish

As you place the food on a small dish, think thoughts of gratitude. Focus your awareness on your breath as you softly hum or sing a song of your choice. Prepare this as if you are giving it to someone you really love, as if your ancestors were still in the physical world. Place the dish on an altar or outside your front door to welcome in the relationship. If you aren't sure what to sing, try singing a song your passed loved one really loved. You can also play music. Whatever you choose, know that you are seen and loved by your loved ones.

Ritual to Activate Cedar

You will need:

Cedar	**Burning pot (metal or clay)**

Start by placing the cedar on your heart. Set an intention by saying one word aloud of what you are calling in. Say the name of the passed loved one whom you are calling in. Then repeat your word by saying, "[*name of passed love one*], I call upon you at this time to activate [*word that you are calling*] in my life at this time." Keep holding the cedar wood at your heart until you actually feel that the word you are seeking is already embodied by you. From this, put the wood into a pot for burning. Light the wood until it creates smoke. From the smoke, walk around a physical place, fan it toward parts of your body, or place it in a designated place. Meditate as the smoke burns and use visualization meditation where you imagine that your loved one is with you and you feel gratitude for this. When you feel complete, wait for the smoke to burn out or smother the ashes to be sure everything is burned out.

Mala Bead Ritual

You will need:

Mala beads

To start using your mala beads to connect with the afterlife, begin with the Sanskrit phrase *Aham Brahmasmi*, which means "totality"—"I am everything, and I cannot be deserted." *Aham Brahmasmi* reminds you that you are spirit and you are human. You are *everything*. It connects you with your highest self and enables you to see the big picture.

Say this phrase softly to yourself 108 times once a day, touching each mala bead in turn. To receive the full effect, do this every morning for 111 days.

Ritual for Asking for Help with a Choice

You will need:

Pendulum   **Pen**

Piece of paper

Using a pendulum can enhance clarity when receiving a direct message from a passed loved one. Begin by thinking of your question. On the piece of paper, draw a semicircle. As if cutting half a pie into three pieces, draw two more lines that meet in the center, creating three even spaces.

Narrow down three potential answers to the question you asked. Write them in the three slices.

Now, holding the pendulum with your left hand, bring it to the center of the edge of the semicircle where the two lines meet. Hold still and draw the point down with the fingers of your right hand so that the pendulum starts off still.

Ask your passed loved one, "Which of these options is for my highest good?"

Remain still and watch the pendulum move. Your answer lies in the direction it points to. If it goes in a circle, ask the question in a different way. If you still don't get an answer, it may not be in your highest good to know the answer at this time.

Ritual to Activate Wealth with Spiritual Support

You will need:

A piece of clear quartz, pyrite, tiger's eye, citrine, or green aventurine

Wealth is described here as living in your divine purpose and being a magnet for everything you want in life. Hold the stone in your left hand and call in your passed loved one. Say aloud, "I see the riches of the world, and the riches see me. I open myself to receive and clear all blockages holding me back from owning my own divine worth destined to me."

Sit in this frequency of being rich until you believe you actually are. This is not about having money; this is an attitude. It is a frequency, a vibration of your highest self. When you notice the feeling of the crystal shift, you are complete.

Place this stone in the far-left corner from the view of your home's entrance. Thank your passed loved one for supporting you and seeing you in your wholeness.

Ritual to Feel Spirit

You will need:

Candle   **Music**
Space to move

Do the candle ritual on page 85. When you set the candle down in front of you, dim the lights, turn on some music that makes you feel good, and start dancing. Dance faster, faster, and faster. Lose your inhibitions, dance like no one is watching, and let yourself go.

When you feel complete, blow out the candle and sit on the floor. Close your eyes and place both hands on your heart and breathe. Connect in and feel Spirit all around you.

Ritual to Say Goodbye

You will need:

Blank paper   **An envelope**

A pen

Take your time with this ritual. Find a comfortable place to sit and write. Before you begin writing, sit up tall and place both hands on your heart. Take a deep breath in and connect with your lost loved one. Hold your heart as if you are holding your entire intensity of love. Take a moment to pause if needed, but allow the memories of this soul here on Earth to come up.

With each passing moment, tell yourself and your passed loved one "Thank you." If forgiveness feels more appropriate, then express that. Keep holding your heart as you allow the emotions to pass through you. Find the realization within yourself that although you will not stop missing this person, the acceptance that they are physically gone will ease your mourning journey.

Start to meditate on the areas of your life that you would like support in. As you say goodbye to your loved one's existence here on Earth, say hello to their spiritual body. This is to transition your mind to seeing that they are a soul with a spirit and their body was temporary.

Grab the pen and paper. Address the page with "Dear [*fill in your loved one's name*]." Slowly form words into content from your heart. Write this letter to transition your passed loved one. Let the words form effortlessly and allow your feeling to be put into words. Let yourself get ugly; let everything go. In the end, write down some requests you have of this spirit body. Close out this letter with sentiments that feel good to you and sign your name.

Put the letter in the envelope. Now release this letter by burning it in a safe, controlled fire, tearing it into pieces, or burying it.

Three Questions Ritual

You will need:

Three small pieces **A voice recorder**
  of paper **or notepad**
A pen **Your journal**

On each of the three pieces of paper, write down one question you want your passed loved one to answer. Remember to be clear with the questions you ask.

Ball up each piece of paper and place the balls in front of you. Now mix them up so you don't know one from the other. Number them 1, 2, and 3. Do not open them until you are completely done with the following steps.

Take a moment to scan your body. Notice how you feel before you begin for comparison. Hold the first ball of paper in your palm. Notice what comes up for you. Does it feel warm, cold, something else? Do you think of someone or a place? Whatever you experience, say it aloud into your recorder or jot it down on a notepad. Do this for the other two balls as well.

When you've completed the sensing part, open each ball, one at a time, and look at the question you asked. Play your recording or look at the notes you took. In your journal, jot down how your questions may have been answered in any way that makes sense to you.

Ritual to Send Love

You will need:

A bouquet of roses (or a different flower you feel called to)

Ocean, lake, or stream (or a drawn bath)

Find a place to sit on the edge of the water. Close your eyes, relax your mind, and become present with where you are. Feel the air on your skin and the light from heaven pouring down upon you. Imagine that this light is a bright beam of beautiful golden rays that lifts your spirit body to meet your passed loved one.

Take a few deep breaths, and then open your eyes and hold one of the flowers. Slowly peel off the petals while capturing and admiring all the beauty of the flower. Take your time, smelling, feeling, and embracing all the aspects of nature.

Hold the loose petals in your hand. Take a breath in and release the petals into the water as you say aloud, "I love you." Repeat this with each offer of petals into the water until you feel complete. Stack both hands over your heart and repeat again, "I love you."

Peace Walk Ritual

You will need:

Walking shoes   **Mala beads (optional)**

This is an intuitive walk for making sure your loved one is at peace. You can do this wherever you want. Start by placing your hand over your heart and feeling your heartbeat. As you connect with your physical body, call in Spirit and all your passed loved ones to walk with you.

Take a deep breath in, and as you release it, see the world as if you were born anew. Repeat the phrase "Peace begins with me" three times before you begin walking. Then head in whichever direction you are guided. As you walk, say, "Peace begins with me." You may start off saying it aloud until you feel called to whisper it and then to say it silently to yourself.

You can use mala beads or your fingertips to follow along. If you are using the mala beads, say the whole phrase once for each bead. If you are using your fingertips, say one word at a time, beginning at your index finger: "Peace." Go to your middle finger and say, "Begins," and so on. Embody the peace you wish for your passed loved one, and experience the heaven they are already in. Repeat this phrase until you fully feel your passed loved one's peace.

CHAPTER 6

Signs from the Other Side

This chapter is an A-to-Z list of common and some more advanced signs from the afterlife. However, it is important to associate your own interpretation with anything that crosses your path. Take time reviewing these entries along with the real-life examples offered and make notes in your journal. Trust yourself, and remember that when communicating with Spirit and connecting with your higher self, there are no coincidences. This chapter is not a comprehensive list. Rather, it is just to get you comfortable noticing the meanings of the signs your loved one may use to communicate with you.

The way each symbol appears is the most important factor to consider when interpreting it. Think outside the box. You know when Spirit is asking you to work with a new symbol because you will see it at least three times or you may feel emotional when you encounter it. When working with a new sign, it is as if Spirit is adding a new word to your vocabulary that only you can interpret the meaning of. This may mean you have repetitive experiences with a specific animal, number, or object. For example, I have seen exactly five broken eggs as I write the last chapter of this book. To me, it symbolizes a new birthing as writing this book has felt very much like an incubating baby and now it is ready to hatch. Five is also the number of shifting and changes.

When we find a symbol to communicate with the afterlife, it doesn't just come down from the sky and clearly state, "Ta-da! I am that symbol you were looking for!" We actually develop symbols as we continue to grow in our spiritual gifts and trust our abilities. You can also ask your loved one to give you a sign, even a specific one. Try it out and see what happens.

There are so many signs out in the world for you to discover. Understand that signs often prompt you to say something out loud or trigger a memory. Sometimes, it is about not the actual sign but the message behind it. For example, I kept seeing a honeycomb with bees around a client. I saw the honey glowing and oozing down. I could place the honeybee around the client. I could feel that her grandmother's name was coming through as Honey. That was the important thing that the spirit wanted to communicate. Read between the lines to hear what your passed loved one is telling you. As you continue using your own symbols, you will learn what they mean, how to respond, and what to take away from the experience.

Apple

Apples represent wisdom. This is a common symbol sent by the afterlife to remind us of the importance of learning and growing. When I'm craving apples, I think about how I can integrate new wisdom into my life.

When we think of an apple, we often think of a red apple, but apples come in many different varieties and forms. Every detail matters when looking at a symbol. The way it is presented to you tells a story. To get the most out of the symbol, notice: How are you experiencing this apple? Is it coming to you in juice form? Is the apple rotten? Does the apple have leaves or stems? Is this a Granny Smith apple, the color green, which can symbolize grandmother or the heart? Do you have memories with apples? The most important question to ask is if this means anything to you.

In many folktales, apples represent death and rebirth, so the apple is also a symbol of fertility. Think of Johnny Appleseed planting seeds all over. When an apple is shown to you, this may be your passed loved one reminding you that they are with you and are helping plant seeds for your future. Or it may be that they want to remind you about growth and learning. So next time you see an apple lying around or envision one in your head, take some time to think if there is some importance.

My client April was going through a hard time after her mother passed, and she was looking for a sign her mother was still with her. She felt called to sit in her local park under a tree to meditate. She closed her eyes and asked for a sign. When she opened her eyes, there was a big apple on a man's T-shirt right in front of her. April was shocked because she had just gotten a unique tattoo of an apple to represent her love for teaching. April had followed in her mother's footsteps and become a teacher; their love for learning was a big connection between them. April had been debating whether to move to a new teaching job. Seeing that apple gave her the courage to move forward in her career.

Bumblebee/Honeybee

A bumblebee or honeybee represents the nectar of life. You may see a honeycomb hive, black and yellow, or an actual bee. In every hive, there is a queen, who is taken care of by the community. Every bee contributes; they know their divine order. Many interpret bees with honey as representing heaven. Even at the altar of St. Peter's Basilica in the Vatican, honeybees wrap around the columns. When you see a honeybee, think of the sweet life and the devotion necessary to receive it. When a bee comes into your life, this symbol relates to productivity and socialization. The bee is also a great omen of abundance.

I had a client, Pam, who told me she got stung on her foot after she had been asking for support from her grandmother. Pam was an accountant who had been working hard all summer long. She feared she wouldn't have enough cash after purchasing her new home. Pam really struggled to accept help, and at work she was known to take on other people's tasks. She sat in a session with me, and right after, she was stung on the foot. It was shocking to her because she knew that her grandmother, who had just come through, was reminding her to be the queen. Being stung on her foot especially meant to her that she was more productive delegating work than taking it all on by herself.

Butterfly

A butterfly represents transformation. To become a butterfly, a caterpillar must go through the process of metamorphosis; it does not suffer and does not judge the process. There are big shifts happening in your life when a butterfly floats by, so know that the butterfly reminds you to be patient with your transformation. See the beauty that you are and the opportunities your life has to offer. Know that your passed loved one is sending you a message of hope; now is the time to spread your wings and fly.

My client Sherrell was visiting family for the holidays. It was her first holiday back after her father had survived his cancer treatments. A lime-green butterfly landed on the back deck and sat with Sherrell as she drank her coffee every morning. On the last day, the butterfly landed on her hand. For her, this was a clear sign from Spirit that she no longer needed to worry about her father's health. He was being protected and was transforming into a more conscious and healthier version of himself.

Cat

The cat is a sacred animal that was worshipped by the ancient Egyptians. They believed cats were magical and treated them with great honor, even mummifying them at death. If your loved one is showing you a cat, you are being acknowledged for your magical qualities. Felines are known for regal independence, so you are being called into independent action at this time. You may be feeling confident within yourself to stand out on your own. Cats can navigate in the darkness. Know there is nothing to fear when a cat shows up. Cats use their flexibility and divine feminine power to thrive through any challenges.

My client Anna wrote to me that she was on her way to run a race when she came across a dead cat. She felt that her passed loved ones were telling her that it was safe to step out on her own and run this race with majestic power and grace. It was no longer time for her to struggle but to enjoy the experience of running this race at her speed.

Cow

The cow represents sacrifice because, for many lifetimes, this animal has been a part of sacrificial rituals. Cows are considered a sacred animal in the Hindu culture, and many refrain from eating beef to honor the sacredness. Of course, with this sacrifice and its nurturing personality, the cow is the mother of all mothers. Cattle have given humanity life-sustaining energy through meat and milk. In Egypt, there is a deity named Hathor who has a cow head and is represented as the first mother. She is known to have activated the first divination. When a cow comes across your path, Spirit is affirming that you are experiencing birth and fertility. You may be called to connect with Mother Earth and to access your nurturing qualities.

Crab

When a crab appears in your life, know that a passed loved one is telling you that evolving does not always mean you have to move forward. Just like the crab that walks sideways, something in your life may feel like you are taking steps back, but look again; you may be further along than you thought.

The crab has a strong shell but is soft on the inside. The spirit pertaining to this message could have been perceived as a bit "crabby" when they were on Earth. This is a spirit telling you that although their feelings may not have always been expressed, they want you to know that they love you very deeply. This can also represent the zodiac sign Cancer and may pertain to a birthday or important date that falls within the time frame of that sign. (Look up the other zodiac symbols as well; seeing their representation may indicate that there's a message for you that pertains to that time of year.)

George was walking on the beach and asked to connect with his grandfather. As he continued his walk, a wave hit the shore, and he almost stepped on the tiniest crab. He knew it was a powerful experience but didn't understand it until he got in his car and remembered that his grandfather's zodiac sign was Cancer, which is represented by a crab.

Calendar Dates

When you repetitively see a special date, this is your passed loved ones reminding you that they are remembering this date. This can be symbolized through the actual date showing up as a date of death, anniversary, or birth date, but it isn't limited to those. The numbers may physically show up in your life on receipts, street signs, license plates, or a clock. When you see your birth date, Spirit is telling you that you are fulfilling your life journey. Anytime your birthday arises in numbers, remember that your passed loved one is confirming the path you are on.

My client Giselle knew she had made the right decision to take a trip to Mexico after her flight number happened to be her birth date. When she got in the taxi to the airport, she looked at the clock; it was an hour behind and set on her birth date. She continued to see her birth date everywhere she went. During this trip to Mexico, she met her future husband.

Dog

Dogs have lived alongside humans since the Stone Age. They are the ultimate companions. If Spirit is bringing in a dog, the message is about loyalty. When a dog comes along your path, know that you are protected and guarded by your passed loved ones. Spirits of dogs often come through if both the owner and their dog have passed.

I was in a session with a man whose friend in life was Lynn. Before her spirit came through, I was presented with an all-white golden retriever. This sign was meant to assure my client that his friend was protected and safe on the other side. He was able to confirm that Lynn actually had a white golden retriever, which had been her devoted companion in life.

Dragonfly

The dragonfly is a symbol of spiritual change. When this insect shows up in your life, it is there to remind you about lightness and joy in your life. A dragonfly sheds its skin many times in its lifetime. Every time it sheds skin, it completely changes. Therefore, this symbol reflects rebirth and adaptability.

Before my client moved to a new city, she was being swarmed with dragonflies. She knew that this was a sign that her sister, who had passed, was supporting her in her move. When her sister showed her the symbol of the dragonfly, she knew her move would bring many new changes into her life.

Elephant

An elephant represents the removal of obstacles, just like an elephant in the forest that easily knocks down trees and clears the way for others. This is a sign that you are being supported by your spiritual team. When an elephant comes to mind or appears to you, know that your passed loved ones are showing you signs of honor, strength, and patience. Elephants are also often seen as good luck, prosperity, and protection.

When my new client Hector went out for a run to calm his nerves, he prayed to his dad to remove the obstacles in his way. Afterward, he met his wife at a restaurant and saw a man with an elephant tattoo on his neck. Later that day, his child showed him his toy elephant. Then his wife tried on her new earrings—sterling-silver elephants. He knew the third sign had to mean something important, so he looked up the meaning and called me. Hector felt this was a message from his dad saying he was holding Hector's problems and Hector could let go of the intense pressure he felt to succeed.

Feather

When a feather crosses your path, know that your passed loved one is looking out for you and that you are taken care of. If the feather is white, angels also surround this issue and all is well. If the feather is black, this may mean that energies that are not for your highest good are now resolved and out of your way.

Different feathers carry different meanings. For example, a crow's feather is a symbol of change coming. A vulture's feather is a symbol of anything that doesn't serve your life falling away because vultures eat the dead. A feather from a green parrot may be reminding you to revisit the dreams you once left behind and to speak your voice. A pigeon's or a dove's feather is a bringer of peace and love. You can learn more about the spiritual meaning of birds and what their feathers may symbolize by doing an Internet search.

Jose started working with me after he moved back to Miami, his birthplace. He returned home after the passing of his father to support his mother. While he was living back in Miami, memories of old dreams he had left behind flooded his heart. Surrounded by family, he was struggling to get by and trying to keep everyone happy. One day, a green parrot feather fell out of a tree and landed at his feet while he was walking his dog. He knew this message was for him; it was time to tell his family how he really felt and to start pursuing his long-forgotten dreams.

Frog

When Spirit brings a frog hopping into your life, you can expect to go far. When a frog crosses your path, your passed loved one is telling you that you are taking a big leap forward. In many cultures around the world, frogs represent fortune. Frogs can also be seen in native art. This symbol represents ancient wisdom, so know that what is coming to you now comes from a deep inner knowing. Trust what feels right and go for it.

My client Terri was gifted vocally and was working on a career as a professional singer. She did not have much time to devote to dating. She had a deep connection with her father, who had passed away. Terri was concerned she would never find a partner if she continued to pursue her singing career. She wrote me an email one day after she was sitting in her backyard speaking about this to her dad in the spirit world. She asked him clearly, "Will I ever find a partner to settle down with?" She turned around, and there in a palm tree were two frogs stacked on top of each other, looking at her with their big frog eyes.

Grasshopper

Grasshoppers are known to be good luck in many different cultures. There are good fortune and abundance around anyone when a grasshopper chooses to join in. This is a sign of freedom and joy. Spirit may be revealing illusions and bringing new insight into your life. This insect symbolizes forward thinking, advanced spiritual powers, and the clear ability to move ahead in life.

Frank came to me seeking confirmation about starting his own spiritual center in a rural area. He had lived in the city for more than seven years and was burned out. The first message I received from his passed loved one was a big green grasshopper. When I shared this, he knew it was time for him to take the next leap of faith.

Hawk

A hawk represents the strength and courage of a warrior. When this bird or bird's feather appears in your life, your passed loved ones are reminding you of the power that exists inside you. The hawk has intuition and higher vision to carry out tasks and make decisions for the greatest good of all. The hawk may come through flying in the sky, catching prey, or gifting you with a feather. A hawk may also be depicted in a photo or art piece. If a hawk crosses your path, know that you have the courage to do the greatest good for all.

A hawk landed in a client's yard while she was sorting her passed grandmother's heirlooms. It was a difficult time to be the one to have the final say on which items belonged to whom, but she followed her heart and did what her grandmother wanted her to do. After the last day of going through her grandmother's house, she returned back home. The next morning, she awoke and found a hawk walking in the grass in front of her house. Her grandmother was thanking her for listening to the higher vision.

Hearts

Hearts are common symbols that the spiritual world uses to communicate. They may be in the iconic shape or the actual physical organ. After a loved one passes, you may notice that hearts pop up throughout your day in random places. You may see an illustration of a heart, or it may come through almost as an illusion. Sometimes you may even see a heart-shaped cloud. When you see a heart, know that your passed loved one is coming through to remind you of their love for you. Feel the love and excitement throughout your day when you see a heart and know that you are supported by Spirit.

After my client Bianca lost her husband, she took up yoga to help her mourn the loss. After her first class, she noticed that the sweat on her yoga mat seemed to be in the shape of a big heart. Every time she showed up to yoga, she kept seeing hearts. Her husband loved yoga, but Bianca had never accompanied him to classes. She knew that these hearts were a sign from him that he was with her.

Letters

Letters you see may come together to form words or initials that may have significant meaning to you. They may appear on billboards, license plates, phones, social media, and many other places. When the initials of a passed love one's name appear, know that their spirit is near. If a spirit shows you your own initials or those of another family member, know that you or they are surrounded in love and protection.

After my client Rebecca lost her baby, she began to see the initials of the baby's name throughout her day. When she returned to work, in her morning commute, the initials would be so loud that she could not ignore the sign. A car would cut her off, and it would have the exact initials of the full name she would have named her child. She knew that her beautiful daughter was watching over her and telling her to keep moving forward in her healing process.

Numbers

The more you open up and study numerology, the more your passed loved ones will use numbers to communicate with you. Every number carries a certain vibration. Spirits often send numbers grouped in threes to confirm that a message has been sent from the spiritual world, but I also invite you to look at each number individually. See the numbers as if they were telling a story. For example, I see the number 7 as a symbol of faith. When I look at the number 7, it looks top-heavy, as if it should fall over, but it stands on its own because it trusts. To me, the number 6 looks like a seed that was planted and is now growing; I also see a pregnant woman. The number 6 is a power number and connects with the ultimate power, the power of love.

Take your time to discover what makes sense to you with regard to numbers. They will appear throughout your day on clocks, phones, receipts, the Internet, license plates, phone numbers, and even street addresses. The following are some of the most common numerical signs our passed loves ones may send to us.

111

The number 111 is a message from passed loved ones that we are aligned with our highest good and are being encouraged to continue to listen. This number is the gateway to the spiritual world. The vibrancy of this number has a high frequency, so know that you are in the right place at the right time. When this number appears, try to understand what is happening at the current time. What conversation were you having with yourself or another person?

222

When 222 shows up in your life, your passed loved ones are teaching you a lesson for your highest good. Two brings in companionship and also life purpose. What you are learning now will be used for the good of the world. Keep staying on the path and know that the wisdom you learn from this experience will help you along your way. This number also comes in to remind you a new path is beginning for you. Stay balanced on this journey, and know that everything is coming together just as it was meant to. This number can also represent partnership, indicating that you are being moved toward someone meaningful in your life.

333

The number of 333 symbolizes your worth. Are you feeling worthy of receiving the abundance of the world? Your passed loved ones are trying to give it to you now. Spirit is coming to you to let you know that your prayers have been heard. You will receive everything you want and more; find the worth inside you to receive it. When 333 appears, your deserving power is increasing. It is time to be extra kind to yourself and ask for what you really want out of life because you will receive it.

444

The number 444 represents a higher vision. Trust that what is being shown to you is truth. Pay attention to your intuition when this number comes through. Know that the decision that needs to be made is from the higher realms because it has already been written in your destiny. See life from the big picture and know that you are protected in all ways by your passed loved ones now.

555

When the number 555 shows up, Spirit is telling you it is time to change or be changed because life is about to start looking different. There is a positive change that will begin to take place soon—try not to resist it. Go with it. Take the time you need for this transition, but have faith that this major shift is here for your greatest good. When the number 555 comes through, there is no need to worry; this life change is a major upgrade from where you are living now. Surrender any expectations you may have at this time so that you can fully receive without any struggle.

888

When the number 888 comes in your life, it represents infinity. This number reminds you that anything is possible when you believe. Your passed loved ones are assuring you that there is always enough for everyone, so steer away from competition or jealousy. Just because your cup is full doesn't mean that another's is empty. Your full cup means that you can fill another cup, and so on. If you shrink to fit in, fearing you have more than others, the world grows darker. Instead, shine your light and let the whole world know who you are. Your loved ones are letting you know that you are provided for now and always. There is nothing to fear, so go out and live in love.

When my client Natalia wrecked her car, she was terrified she wouldn't have enough money to cover the cost because it wasn't covered by insurance. When she turned in the car for repairs, the number on the tag that identified her car on the lot was 888. She knew all would be well and even got two extra clients that day, and those fees covered the cost.

Penny

Pennies are placed in your path from a passed loved one who is sending you a message of appreciation. This symbol is a great reminder that everything is going to be all right. Pennies bring good fortune and remind you that luck is on your side. Wherever a penny shows up for you, know that there are no coincidences. Your passed loved one is sharing a message with you to believe in what you are doing. In some New Year's traditions, pennies are spread out at the front door of a home to bring in good luck, wealth, and happiness for the new year. Through pennies and other change (such as dimes, quarters, and bills), Spirit is reminding you of the prosperity that already exists in your life. Know that Spirit is reminding you of the good fortune you already are; know that there is more to come.

My client Brianna arrived at the airport and realized she had accidentally packed her expensive shampoo in her carry-on. Her bag went through the scanner and was flagged by airport security. She surrendered to the situation, clearly knowing the rules of TSA and thinking for sure her shampoo would be confiscated. As she walked over to the TSA agent, she noticed a penny on the floor. Knowing this coin was a symbol from her father, who had recently passed, she smiled and said softly to herself, "Surprise me." Brianna stood in front of her bag waiting to lose her shampoo when suddenly a celebrity came through the line with a full security pass. The agent checking her bag looked in it briefly and hastily handed it over to Brianna as she left to attend to the chaos surrounding the celebrity. Brianna stood in pleasant disbelief.

Rainbow

Your passed loved one sends rainbows to remind you of the promise of love that is always available in your life. Rainbows come after the storm when everything is cleansed. There are many colors in the rainbow, and they need each other to complete it. True abundance comes from sharing. A rainbow brings a message to let others into your life. Just like a rainbow, we shine brighter when we shine together. Receive support and give others opportunities to show what color they can add to your life. True love is all around you. It is in the water, the trees, and the ocean. See the love that exists and know that you are it.

Rebecca was devastated after the loss of her baby daughter, who had passed away during a complication in labor. During her mourning process, Rebecca's friends and family knew how much she wanted another baby, even after the devastating loss. Anytime they saw a rainbow, they would post a picture on social media and tag her in it. People from the local community caught on and heard about Rebecca's story. People from all over the world started tagging her in their pictures of rainbows. When she became pregnant again, the community of support and love had grown worldwide. Rebecca went into labor with so much support and felt at peace knowing that her first baby girl was there supporting the process.

Rose

A rose represents love of all kinds. Different-color roses can be perceived in a variety of ways. When a spirit hands over a rose to someone, they are doing so out of affection. The deeper the color of the rose, the more passionate this relationship is. The thorns on the rose are a reminder that it is safe to have an edge and still be beautiful. When a passed loved one sends you a Valentine's Day–like rose, this may be pointing to events around the month of February.

During my client Phillip's session, when I connected to his father, I saw that his father had a rose in his hand for Phillip's life partner. This was a symbol of love and honor for the man who had taken care of his son, and although his father had been unable to accept his son for being gay on Earth, he came back carrying a rose to convey his love and appreciation for his son and his partner.

Snake

When a snake slithers your way, your passed loved one is telling you it is time to shed your skin. A coiled serpent is a symbol for kundalini, a Sanskrit term that means "energy rising." This energy is coiled at the base of the spine, and when it rises, you connect with the spiritual world. An ancient symbol, snakes are still represented today on the caduceus, the traditional symbol of Hermes and better known as the symbol of medicine. This symbolizes a rising frequency. When we live with the snake coiled, we live in a depressed state. Keep moving upward, and all will fall into place. Whenever Spirit sends you a snake or a symbol of one, the message indicates rebirth.

When Charlie was just starting his business, he went to pump gas and noticed that a piece of skin from a snake had gotten caught in his side window. He was mourning the loss of his mother and had invested his inheritance in his business. When he received the snake symbol, he knew that his mother was there supporting his decision to expand his business.

Turtle

A turtle is an ancient symbol that Spirit sends to you when you are ready to find home. The turtle represents Mother Earth because when the turtle comes into your life, Spirit is reminding you that your home travels with you wherever you go. The turtle is a symbol of good health and the message that a slow race can be just as successful as one that is rushed. Go at your own pace and know that all will happen in divine timing. Just like the divine mother lets things come to her, there is always enough time. Life is not meant to be rushed; slow your pace and let life be lived through your internal compass.

Woodpecker

A woodpecker comes across your path when Spirit is telling you it is time to find a rhythm to life. Spirit uses a woodpecker to announce that opportunity is on the horizon. Keep moving at a steady rhythm, and you will receive what you are looking for. The red head of some woodpeckers speaks to the mental health and internal clock within our minds. The woodpecker indicates that balance is an important factor; be sure to include both work and play in your daily schedule.

Sara emailed me a video of a woodpecker living in her attic. After our session, she found him there building away. She knew right away that the woodpecker had been sent by her aunt Lucy, who had passed. Her aunt had struggled to create routine and balance in her life while she was alive. Sara had the bird carefully removed and thanked her aunt Lucy for reminding her to make enough time in her day to have some fun. Sara had recently adopted two boys and was not making time for herself. Her aunt Lucy came back through the woodpecker to demand that Sara take more time for herself.

Seeing the messages in the signs and symbols that your loved one puts in your path only works if you believe in yourself. Understand that the world is here to serve you and provide you with lessons to help you evolve. When you shine your light in the world, people want to draw closer to you for warmth.

Conclusion: Believe and Receive

A broken heart is where the light comes in. Grief is growth in disguise. Let yourself not get lost in the circumstances but rise from them. The power within you is stronger than anything that happens to you. You are more powerful than your loss or any circumstances in your life. This grief is here to serve you so that you may see the power you are. Light up the world and share your wisdom. This is your time to free the world by first freeing yourself. Continue on this path and know that this wisdom will never leave you. Be the person who believes in magic, the signs, and the messages. The universe is here to serve you, one heartbeat at a time.

In a 1903 essay called "Optimism," Helen Keller wrote, "Although there is a world full of suffering, it is full also of the overcoming of it." You are not alone in your healing process, no matter how real that may feel at times. There are many who have felt the heartbreak of loss and have overcome it. There are those who have turned their limitations into their assets. Think of the impact people like Harriet Tubman, Mahatma Gandhi, Martin Luther King Jr., Nelson Mandela, Albert Einstein, and Stephen Hawking had on the world after experiencing incredible limitations. Just imagine how different the world would be if they had quit when life challenged them. Each of these powerful leaders befriended their circumstances and welcomed the challenges. Their misfortunes became a part of their story of how they made lasting change in the world.

Life gives you lessons to serve your highest self. We are given limitations to overcome them to create more space for possibility. We can only see the light when we have been in darkness. Life begins in the womb, the darkest place known to humans. This is where seeds sprout. So when life gets you down, remember that this is a gift. You are being challenged so that you may rise again and shine brighter than you ever have before.

For us to find comfort in the uncomfortable we must befriend silence. We must befriend pain. Both are temporary because everything is temporary. That is the beauty of life. It is a giant wheel that forever turns. The only permanent thing is change. Although the calm waters feel peaceful, it is in the storm where we find our depth. Be a rider of the storm because you have nothing to fear. You are more powerful than your emotions and your circumstances. If you learned anything from this book, I hope you understand how powerful you are. You are not here to follow the pack; you are here to create a new way. It is time to listen to your passed loved ones and to be moved by your emotions.

We will never have world peace until we first embody it in our hearts. The way to peace is through listening and learning how to ride the storm. Listen to the signs and messages. Create rituals in your life that serve you. Come back to this book as you need. This wisdom will always be here. It cannot be forgotten.

Resources

Websites

Forever Family Foundation
ForeverFamilyFoundation.org

National Association for the Education of Young Children (NAEYC), "Resources on Death for Young Children, Families, and Educators"
NAEYC.org/resources/topics/coping-stress-and-violence/resources-death

Books

Kübler-Ross, Elisabeth. *On Grief and Grieving: Finding the Meaning of Grief Through the Five Stages of Loss*. New York: Scribner, 2014.

Levine, Peter A. *Waking the Tiger: Healing Trauma*, illustrated edition. Berkeley, CA: North Atlantic Books, 1997.

van der Kolk, Bessel. *The Body Keeps the Score: Brain, Mind, and Body in the Healing of Trauma*, illustrated edition. New York: Penguin Books, 2015.

Weiss, Brian L. *Many Lives, Many Masters: The True Story of a Prominent Psychiatrist, His Young Patient, and the Past-Life Therapy That Changed Both Their Lives*. New York: Fireside, 1988.

Index

M

Mala beads, 81, 91, 99

Mantra chanting, 73, 81

Meditation
cedar use for, 90
communication of Spirit
during, 35, 37, 40, 72–73
grief meditation, 10
"hold the power" technique, 45
meditation beads, 81
moving meditation and
intentional breathwork, 83

Mediumship
connections with spirit,
closing down, 56
crystals, holding during
energy exchanges, 82
the dead, communicating
with, 2, 61–62, 65
energy healing during sessions, 16
inheritance of psychic abilities, 38
who comes through, no choice in, 27

Messages, 8, 43, 55
astrological messages, 107
belief in, 123, 124
candle messages, 85–86, 87, 88
communication from Spirit,
1–2, 41, 56, 61
general message examples, 67–68
intention setting to receive
messages, 47
meditation as gateway to, 35, 40
passed loves ones, messages
from, 2, 52, 63, 72, 110
pendulums, direct messages
received through, 92
physical form, messages coming in, 42
prayers to receive clear
messages, 35, 45, 46, 50
signs, the messages behind, 102
songs, messages coming
through, 58–59

spirit orb communications, 64
symbols, messages sent through, 62
synchronicity, messages
revealed via, 51
threes, messages sent in, 101, 115

Mourning, 23, 33, 71
altars as designated places
to mourn, 77, 79
beginning to heal, 3, 24
commitment to mourning
period, 74–75
crystals to ease mourning, 82
expected losses, impact of, 9
goodbye ritual, 95
grief and, 20, 21–22
high frequency, maintaining
while mourning, 39–41
memories of loved ones, 19, 31
mourning process, empowering, 86
processing feelings of, 15–16
sacredness of mourning, 4
shiva as the Jewish
mourning period, 30
signs delivered during
mourning, 114, 121
sudden loss, reactions to, 8

N

Number symbolism
5 as the number of change, 102, 117
7 as a symbol of faith, 115
111 as gateway to the spiritual
world, 115–116
222 and lessons for your
highest good, 116
333 as symbolizing your worth, 116
444 as representative of
higher vision, 117
555 as announcing major shifts, 117
888 and the power of
belief, 117–118
numbers on the clock, 62, 108, 115

About the Author

Audrey Sloan Tate is a second-generation spiritual medium and mentor currently living in Miami, Florida. She is most well known for her development classes and workshops online. She is a 500-hour yoga teacher trainer and Holy Fire Reiki Master. Audrey Sloan has studied mediumship at the world-renowned Arthur Findlay College. She is passionate about transforming mental illness into spiritual powers.